In the Mystic Footsteps of Saints
VOLUME 1

Grandshaykh Abd Allah Ad Daghestani (ق), with his successor,
Shaykh Nazim Adil Al Haqqani (ق) (1957).

© 2002 Naqshbandi Haqqani Sufi Order

Naqshbandi Haqqani Sufi Order
17195 Silver Parkway #206
Fenton MI 48430 USA
Telephone (810) 714 7007
Facsimile (810) 963 0639
www.naqshbandi.org
staff@naqshbandi.org

The Naqshbandi Haqqani Sufi Order is a non profit, US based organization dedicated to spreading traditional Islamic spirituality and teachings.

Please visit www.naqshbandi.org for more titles in Islamic spirituality and traditional scholarship.

ISBN: 1 930409 05 2

Table of Contents

Can You Tell a Diamond From a Piece of Glass?

"Speak in accordance with peoples' understanding."

That is the advice of the Prophet Muhammad, peace be upon him, to everyone in the world who is trying to communicate with another person. In trying to make someone understand what you are saying you must perceive on what level this is possible and meet him there. There is no benefit in trying to teach first graders calculus nor in teaching university students addition and subtraction.

During the holy Prophet's night journey and his ascension through the seven heavens to the Divine Presence, Allah Almighty bestowed upon him divine knowledge, and He taught the Prophet that there are three distinct categories into which this knowledge is divided. The first category of knowledge taught to him was to be shared commonly with all mankind. None of this knowledge is going to shock or disturb people: it is clear and straightforward, can be easily understood by even the simple mind, and it is expressed in a way peoples' minds can easily grasp. For example, when I tell you a tale I try to make sure that its contents correspond to your own experiences so that you may benefit from it.

It is one of the miracles of the holy Quran that everyone who reads it may understand something from what he has read: it is not so cryptic or unclear that people should say: "I can't understand." But don't imagine that the meaning of the holy Quran is only what you have understood and no more! Even scholars must be careful not to make such an assumption, for the more we improve in our faith the sharper our minds become. The light of faith brightens our understanding.

If we can understand that our understanding increases only with faith, then we will never raise objections if we find anything in the holy Quran that seems to conflict with what we see to be our better judgment. We must not draw hasty conclusions, but wait until enough of the holy Quran's limitless meanings are revealed to our minds to understand the wisdom in what we read, for the Quran contains Meaning Oceans and we must undergo training to be able to extract pearls from them. And before we assume that we know better than the Quran, or even that we know better than any person, we must pay heed to our Lord's declaration: "Above every knower there is one who knows more", and understand that our perception may be clouded, and that surely there exist people who are more knowledgeable and wise than we are. If common people and scholars alike heed this Quranic observation and understand that others may see and know what they don't or can't know, then they will keep an open mind, and at least not attack those whose knowledge is of a different realm.

The second category of knowledge the holy Prophet was instructed to reveal to initiates, to seekers of truth, in accordance with their thirst for deeper understanding. This knowledge was only for those who had become suitable recipients for extraordinary revelation that would only shock or confuse the uninitiated.

One great grandshaykh, Shaykh Muhyuddin ibn al Arabi, may Allah bless him, received huge grants of knowledge of this category from the holy Prophet. He was one of the first to put into writing knowledge that had previously been passed on orally and spiritually. As a result of this he was widely persecuted. Scholars were scandalized by his writings and said: "From where is he bringing these things: We have looked through the holy Quran and the traditions of the holy Prophet but find nothing in them to support such heretical views." This they were saying in the spirit of those who, in his time, rejected the prophethood of Muhammad, peace be upon him.

From where did that understanding come to Shaykh Muhyuddin? The holy Prophet once said: "Beware of the perception of the true believer, for he sees with the light of Allah." It was the light of strong faith, and the resulting clarity of perception and sharpness of intellect that enabled Shaykh Muhyuddin to delve into the "restricted area." So, if you consider yourself to be a seeker of truth, don't be lazy or timid in your quest, but seek to benefit from the clues provided by those who received initiation into this second category of knowledge. Don't be surprised that Shaykh Muhyuddin, Mawlana Rumi, Abu Yazid al Bistami, Shah Naqshband or Grandshaykh Daghestani reveal knowledge that is beyond the pale of the outward or apparent understanding of Islam. But don't try to force such an understanding on those who are not seeking it, for it is not intended for all. Even the companions of the Prophet, who loved him intensely and were always ready to sacrifice everything for him, were not all able to receive knowledge of this type, and among those who were, some could receive more than others. Sayyidina Ali, the cousin and son in law of the Prophet, was one of those who received the most in depth knowledge; he once said to some of the other companions: "There are two categories of knowledge I received from the holy Prophet: one I reveal to you, and the other, were I to even intimate something of it, you would try to kill me."

Whoever encounters a jewel but knows not the distinguishing characteristics of gems may think it to be part of a fossilized coke bottle and throw it away. There is a famous diamond in Istanbul, perhaps one of the biggest and most valuable diamonds in the world. The story of this diamond may help illustrate my point. That diamond was originally found in a dustbin by a street sweeper. He put it in his pocket and brought it to a spoon maker he knew. The spoon maker saw that it could be valuable, so he offered the street sweeper a wooden spoon in exchange for the diamond. The street sweeper was very happy with the trade, as in those days it was a sign of distinction to carry a spoon in one's belt, and to always be prepared in case rice or soup was served.

Then the spoon maker took the diamond to a jeweler, who paid him a lot of money for it. The jeweler polished it and notified the Vizier about the existence of an extraordinary diamond. The Vizier bought it for a fortune and presented it to the Sultan, who had never seen its like. But to the street sweeper its worth was equivalent only to one wooden spoon.

So, everyone receives what he needs on his level, and this was a divine order to the Prophet: "Give to those who may receive", and it is written on the Preserved Tablet who will be eligible for that knowledge.

The third category of knowledge is that which is between Allah and His prophet to the exclusion of all others. This is the realm of the private confidence bestowed upon the Prophet by his Lord, and it is a depth of knowledge that distinguished him from and sets him above all of the saints and learned people of his nation.

Once we have understood this division of Islamic knowledge into three categories, and especially if we are faithful enough to develop penetrating vision and a share of esoteric knowledge, it should not be difficult for us to address people in accordance with their understanding. In his time the holy Prophet was working mostly with a very coarse and unlearned class of people, and he addressed them accordingly, in a manner suited to their mentality. He built their understanding, so to speak, from the bottom up, laying a strong base upon which to build; but for those of them whose hearts were receptive, their simple origins were no obstacle to their receiving grants of inner knowledge.

In his time, the holy Prophet also addressed more learned people: delegations of Christian clergy from Yemen and Jewish Rabbis and scholars residing in Medina. He addressed them on their respective levels too, discussing his mission in accordance with the contents of their holy Books. But knowledge of religious scripture is neither a condition for, nor a disqualification from inner knowledge – the only condition is a receptive heart and mind, and the only disqualification is pride and envy. So those who came with sincerity and open hearts received amply, but those who came with prejudice could not be helped.

Our time also has its particular conditions and peoples. Certain words or methods may be acceptable to you but difficult for others. When the holy Prophet applied this wisdom to his manner of approaching people, Islam spread both East and West quickly. Therefore, don't be oblivious to the reactions of these who you address, don't run up against a wall, gaining nothing in the process except a bump on the head. Find common ground, then build on it step by step.

Islam derives its vitality from its inherent simplicity and universal principles. The basics may be practiced by all, irrespective of distinctions based on race, nationality, sex, age or cultural adherence, and it is in harmony with nature – with the nature of man and with that of the earth. But we must be worthy of understanding this and communicating it.

In our time elderly people may often be hard on youth for the way they behave, saying: "We never behaved so badly even when we were young." But they must remember under what conditions and social norms those children are now being brought up. Similarly, practicing Muslims who are scrupulously observing the Law of Islam, may be impatient with those who are slowly approaching Islam or whose hearts are drawn to a circle of believers, expecting those people to conform quickly. If this is the case, it is a sign that you have not yet understood anything, and that your practices are only blinders. If you are wise, you will expect or demand only very little in the way of conformity from newcomers. Don't try to load your burden on them – and if you are trying to shift your burden you must consider its causes. Don't worry about bringing people "in line" but rather concern yourself with making sure that your own practices are becoming a means for attaining inner peace and are not becoming an end in themselves. If your practice brings you inner peace and wisdom others will emulate those practices voluntarily.

The proper attitude is indicated in a saying of the holy Prophet: "Make things easy for people, not difficult; give them good tidings and don't drive them away." Now, most Muslims are only driving Westerners farther away from Islam by ignoring the differences in the conditions they face. Such an attitude is a sign that they have deprived themselves of access to that second category of knowledge – wisdom – which brings with itself profound and penetrating vision; indeed, the blind are not even able to understand the first category of knowledge correctly. We ask our Lord to grant us understanding of the Way of Islam, and to help us know in which direction we must go.

The Final Limit: Assemble for the Love of God

One of the main benefits of sitting in the association of a shaykh is that attending such meetings gives more power to our faith and leads to familiarity and feelings of brotherhood with those who attend that association. The attainment of familiarity is a miracle in itself, as our egos are usually too proud to put themselves on the same footing with anyone else. Each ego sees itself as being unique and incomparable. Just as a king must be alone on his throne, so our egos envision themselves at an exalted station.

The ancient Egyptians worshipped many gods and goddesses, but Pharaoh (the contemporary of Moses) tried to abolish the worship of all of these, that he alone might be established as the most worshipable deity. Therefore, in the holy Quran he is quoted as saying to his people: *"I am your Lord Most High."*

In making this statement Pharaoh was acting as spokesman for all egos, and you can't find anyone without such an ego – its characteristics have not changed since the time of Pharaoh.

During the holy Prophet's night journey (in which he was taken by the Angel Gabriel from Mecca to Jerusalem and subsequently on a miraculous journey through the seven heavens), the Lord addressed him, saying: "Oh My servant, oh My beloved Muhammad, if I were to give everyone the opportunity of power and authority alike unto Pharaoh's, all would be Pharaohs and would proclaim 'I am your Lord Most High'. Therefore, teach them to be careful of their egos' tricks, and warn them not to blame anyone, not even Pharaoh."

We must heed the teachings of our Lord and rise above the common level of perception. Pointing the finger and saying, "What a tyrant!" is the common level. If we learn the lesson of our Lord we will come to understand that our own egos are all potential Pharaohs. It is only that destiny has not apportioned us the circumstances for the development of such extreme ego indulgence. But no doubt your ego given half a chance would establish itself on that throne of blasphemy. Therefore, we must be ashamed to say: "That person doesn't pray", or "That person transgresses the Law of God."

Any meeting assembled for the sake of God and in the love of God draws the mercy of God upon us, and helps us to reach our goals. Such is the divine pleasure bestowed upon such a meeting, that even a passerby who happens in out of curiosity and never returns again must ultimately benefit from the mercy that flowed through that meeting to him. What distinguishes such a meeting from others? Only that it is held for the love of God and not for any other motive. You have not come here to eat and drink – that you can do in your countries, but the love of God has called you here. You have begun to hearken to that call, but for most people it is an unnoticed voice in the innermost recesses of their hearts.

Our lives pass before our eyes like a fleeting vision. We are trying to grasp the moment, but every breath flees in exhalation, and the one that is in front of us is soon behind. A car moves down the motorway "swallowing" a mile or more of road a minute, and so pass our lives. We can't hold on to the past, and as we anticipate the future it has already met us and flown by. Life is like a dream. Can you keep anything you saw in a dream? You may dream that you are sitting on a throne with a crown on your head, surrounded by piles of treasure, but you can't take the treasures with you when you open your eyes, nor will anyone treat you like a king even if you tell them that you dreamed it. Where is that dream now? How? What? It was just with me! We must, therefore, not allow our egos to convince us that we are kings with crowns on thrones in treasure filled rooms! But our temporary lives have a serious purpose: spiritual development. That is our task, and a very serious one. Either we take spiritual development with us from this life or else we go empty handed – and no one can improve or develop except by joining the caravan of prophets and saints.

I have met so many people here in the West who have delved deeply into the great traditions of the East. They have acquired wisdom through seeking it. They have read, traveled, listened and learned. The attraction for everything oriental is a divine inspiration in the hearts of Western people: even the ancient Greek philosophers took their light from the East.

But as for Westerners who often subject themselves to great hardships to travel to Tibet and India, and receive wisdom to take back with them, most are in danger losing all they gained. Why? Because they bring back loose pearls. If a lady buys pearls does she carry them loose in her pocket, or does she string them on a strong thread? People are going to great lengths to seek wisdom and are so happy with what they have gained, but all the time the pearls are falling out the holes in their pockets, because the pearls are not yet bound on a thread. What is the thread I am referring to? Wisdom pearls may only be kept with a strong faith and method. So many people have overlooked this necessity. If you have the thread, one by one you may obtain the pearls and string them.

You must follow the methods prescribed by a great religion. I am not going to tell you that you must follow this one or that; all I am saying is that making a hodge podge is useless. Why? Keeping to the precepts of a world religion, without being a fanatic, guards your string of pearls. There are many thieves at work, and you must keep it carefully lest it be stolen. Therefore, faith and wisdom need protection, and you must learn what actions or practices may protect your treasures from thieves. Who tries to go the path alone will wander into a den of thieves, or be attacked by a pack of wolves in no man's land.

To Each His Own Desserts

Allah Almighty has established natural laws, and has bestowed upon us minds with which to understand these laws and their applications. Fire burns, so don't put your hand in fire. Knives cut, so don't put your hand under a knife and trust in God's mercy, no. The same applies to the relationship between rulers and their subjects.

"Don't throw yourselves (foolishly) to your destruction," warns the Almighty. There is always a correct way of dealing with the ruling authorities, and the key to understanding the correct approach is the tradition of the holy Prophet, peace be upon him: *"You get the ruler you deserve."*

Hajjaj bin Yusuf was one of the most famous tyrants of history. "The Tyrant" was his title and a title well earned, as every time he entered a city he made hills from the heads of the people he killed. Once Hajjaj conquered a city and summoned a group of prominent citizens, asking them, "Am I an oppressor or a just ruler?" Naturally those people were quaking with fear, and humbly addressed him: "Oh our Amir, you are very just." He shouted angrily: "They are liars, take them out of my sight and behead them!"

Then Hajjaj called in another contingent of prominent citizens and asked them the same question, but as they understood what had happened to the previous group they said: "How can you be called just when you kill the very people who declare you to be just? Surely you are a tyrant!" "Liars, all of them! They lie too! Executioner, take them away and behead them too!"

And so it continued throughout the day: a group was called, and answered, "You are just" and was killed; then another group who answered, "There has never been a tyrant the likes of you," was killed as well. Gradually all of the prominent citizens of the town were slaughtered, except for a group of religious scholars who Hajjaj was intending to question last.

As they were walking towards their dreaded meeting with Hajjaj, an ecstatic madman of God came up to them and asked them where they were going. "Go away," they answered. "We have no time to talk to you now." "Tell me where you're going," he insisted, "to a banquet? I am going with you!" And so he sauntered from side to side of the group, bothering them and pushing himself upon them.

Finally, one very old shaykh said to him: "Oh my son, leave us, we are going to a slaughterhouse." "Oh let me come too! After slaughtering there should be a feast with plenty of meat!" "As you like," said the old shaykh. Then the madman took a stick and went out in front of the group of scholars like the leader of a marching band.

In this manner they arrived at the court of Hajjaj. Hajjaj was sitting like a frowning statue when the bizarre madman entered with the scholars. Hajjaj was taken aback by the appearance of the madman and a little afraid, as his clothes were weird and his turban was awry. The madman shouted: "Hey, Hajjaj!" The hearts of the scholars fell, and they thought: "My God! No one has ever dared address Hajjaj like this! How did we end up being led here by this madman who is bound to make Hajjaj even angrier. Perhaps he will not just kill us now, but flay us alive!"

The madman continued: "I am the commander of this group of scholars. Don't tire yourself by asking them questions one by one, just ask me what you will. If you are pleased with my answers, fine and well, and if you are not, take them off and slaughter them." Then Hajjaj said to the madman: "Alright, I accept. I will ask you my questions and you will answer for them. Am I an oppressor or a just ruler?" "God forbid that you are an oppressor or a just ruler! You are the ruler sent upon us in accordance with our own attributes. You are a punishment, the curse of God, upon these people. We are the real oppressors, not you."

Then Hajjaj applauded, saying: "All you have said is true. This is the answer I have been waiting for. All day long I have been listening to lies. They called me an oppressor, but no, it is they who are liars, and when the others called me just they were even more shameless. Yes, I am Allah's punishment for their actions. Now I have my answer, you may all go free."

Be wise and learn from this tale. If you think that a government is oppressive, look at the people being ruled and you will understand why they are suffering.

"I Was a Hidden Treasure...."

Allah Almighty has said through His holy words: *"I was a Hidden Treasure and I wanted to be known, so I created this whole creation that it may know Me."*

Pay heed to these words for although this is a brief statement, through it the Creator explains much about Himself, His creation and the purpose of Life. He says that He was, is and always will be a hidden treasure, a treasure without limits, and that He willed a creation into being, worthy of receiving endless grants of His knowledge. Such a Lord may grant endlessly, but even such munificence does not mean that His creatures have encompassed any part of His reality. We are fortunate to pertain to such a Creator and to glorify One whose majesty is eternal and limitless, whose grants – described to us in their differing aspects as power, beauty, mercy, wisdom, knowledge and penetrating will – are constantly renewed so that our souls imbibe ever fresh and invigorating refreshment.

Man was created in the heavenly realm, then he and his wife were sent to live on earth. Allah Almighty sent man into this abode of temporality, but He sent paradise with him. Who was paradise for? Adam and Eve. If the Lord had not sent our mother Eve with our father Adam, he would have exploded like a bomb, but he was able to console himself and find happiness, even in this abode of suffering, with his wife.

When Adam came to this earth, his Lord sent the knowledge of the heavenly realm with him – the very memory of it as a reality. Adam was empowered to establish a spiritual transmission to his descendants, but it soon became necessary to endow another man with a direct glimpse of that reality, so Seth was chosen as a recipient of prophetic revelation, and his spiritual power became a tributary to the original stream established by Adam. But, in fact, Seth received doubly, as what he inherited from Adam was then also his, as well as what he received directly. Then came Enoch (Idris), and in succeeding generations one hundred and twenty four thousand prophets were granted direct revelation streams to feed into the huge river of divine Light coming to them from earlier prophets.

Some people may ask why Allah Almighty sent so many prophets. Our Lord sent them because He loves to grant His servants gifts from His divine knowledge, beauty, mercy, wisdom, power and penetrating will endlessly. As He said, He wants to make Himself known.

And even though the succession of prophethood has spiraled to a climax, first with the advent of Jesus Christ, and then with the mission of the seal of prophets, Muhammad (peace be upon them all), whose duty it was to establish divine Light throughout the world in a unified, universal way not possible in the earlier stages of the development of mankind, don't think that access to divine knowledge is cut off. Never! The prophets of God have always been the leaders of spiritually illumined people on earth, those who have been given the task of guiding initiates and mankind at large. Every one of them brought spiritual energy to this world, energy that did not leave this realm when they did, but remained as a beacon of light through the obscurity of this life. This light is not, as it were unembodied, but incorporated in at least one spiritual heir in every period of human history.

If a person seeks truth, Allah will lead him to such a beacon, to a meeting with an inheritor of a prophet, whose particular guidance qualities suit his potentialities. These inheritors are connected spiritually with the prophets whom they represent and, consequently, when you meet them and are prepared to receive the transmission, you may receive a "photocopy" in your spiritual body and establish direct contact with that prophet – you will be invited to his assembly.

Once Moses was on Mount Sinai conversing with his Lord and addressed Him, saying "Oh my Lord, have any of your servants been honored with such intimate discourse as I have?" The Lord replied: "Oh Moses, have a look around you." Moses looked around and saw the whole valley filled with Moseses, all with long beards and staffs, looking at him as he looked back at them in amazement. Then the Lord addressed him: "Oh Moses, this is only a selection: there are more, but I only show you this small group to give you an idea of what power I have sent through you to the world." He is Almighty Allah, certainly it is no great thing for Him to grant those who sincerely want to be like Moses, and follow in his footsteps, a spiritual power that emanates from Allah but comes to them through Moses.

During the night journey of the Prophet Muhammad and his ascension to the seven heavens, the Angel Gabriel accompanied him part of the way, through the seven heavens, but at a certain point stayed back in awe of the radiance of the divine countenance, fearing to approach further lest he burn. The holy Prophet then ventured on alone and was shown by his Lord a huge gathering of people, also identical to himself, and the Lord told him:

"These are the saints of your nation and my servants: And no one knows the armies of the Lord except Him. Whoso steps in your footsteps will partake of your honor and light."

Therefore, a grandshaykh sitting with his murids must be a means for those murids to attain light from the Prophet whom that grandshaykh represents. It is impossible for a grandshaykh to leave even the weakest of his murids without a share of that power, so that he should attain to the same degree and honor as his grandshaykh.

We have waded into an ocean of deep and secret knowledge, and as it is secret we are being signaled back to shore by the "lifeguard" lest we all drown.

Seek Your Sustenance

The holy Prophet advised his nation to work for a living, though our stay in this world is only temporary. He advises us to seek out our sustenance, not to wait for it to find us. It is best for us to work for our livelihood, to engage ourselves in any type of work that does not transgress the Law, as the most tasteful of food is that earned with one's own hands. For man to seek his sustenance within the bounds of the divine Law is most pleasing to our Lord, and is also conducive to good mental and physical health. So whoever is able bodied must work. Don't argue that, since the sustenance of every creature is already destined for him you need neither pursue it nor avoid it – these are the excuses of lazy people – and Allah does not favor laziness. As long as you are in this world there must be some work that you can do with your hands.

King Solomon, who was both a prophet and a divinely Ordained Monarch was granted by his Lord opulence far beyond the imagination of even the richest man of our time, for Allah Almighty granted him knowledge of the exact location of all the treasures in the earth, and also empowered him over armies of Jinn who not only guarded those treasures but would bring up any of them upon command. Solomon was also granted the power to discourse with the animals, and they too were his servants.

Even such a magnificent emperor as Solomon never in his life ate food except the proceeds from the sale of baskets he himself wove. Can we find such scrupulousness anywhere? King Solomon set an example for all of his subjects, and people of all time by not using the wealth of the nation for his personal needs. But nowadays, on the contrary, the government is expected to supply everyone's needs, so that many people, other than those who are truly handicapped or in need, unashamedly take government handouts and demand that they be increased. Don't be unemployed! Perhaps you can cheat the government, but you can't deceive Allah; and He Almighty punished such people in this life by making that money a cause of discontent for them. No "barakah" comes from unearned money, and the result of such a life will be both physical and mental illness. Therefore, if you value your health and your sanity, eat from the work of your hands!

Sultan Abdul Hamid, the last Khalifah of the Ottoman Empire, was a great personality of his time. By virtue of his great stamina and charisma he was able to not only hold together the crumbling empire, but to actually effect a kind of revival of spirit throughout the vast realm. He was the last ruler to be mentioned in sermons all across the Muslim World, and he was the last keeper of the holy relics of the Prophet that are in Istanbul.

In the midst of all the affairs of his empire that needed his attending to, he found time to engage in a craft and eat from the proceeds of that work. Not only this, but he never ascended his throne to attend to court until he had recited his Naqshbandi exercises and read a portion of the Quran and also of the prayer book 'Dalail ul Khairat", as well as praying the two sets of supererogatory prayers of the early morning. It is enough of a testimony to his strength to mention that he sat on the throne for thirty three years in a time when most kings could not manage to retain their power for even ten years because of the many intrigues and the growing chaos of the times. The magnitude of his majesty was such that Kaiser Wilhelm II once said: "I have met many monarchs and rulers in my life and have found them all to be my inferiors, or at best my equals, but when I entered the presence of Abdul Hamid I began to tremble."

The holy Prophet once said: "You must work for your honest provision as if you are going to remain in this world forever, and for the afterlife as if you will die tomorrow." Now why would the Prophet, whose mission it was to call to eternal life, suggest that we work as if we will always be in this world? Because when hope for the life of the world is abandoned man will die. Hope for the future of this world and for our position in it is necessary for our being able to devote ourselves to our duties in this life. Besides this, the holy Prophet declared that man's good deeds live on after him in this world, through the benefit that future generations derive from them.

And with regard to the afterlife, the holy Prophet was reminding us that we will cross that barrier, and it could be tomorrow, or even today: So, should we not be prepared? In order to put the matter in perspective, the holy Prophet also said: "Oh people, you must consider how long you may remain in this world and work for it in accordance with the length of your stay; and you must consider as well how long you will be in the life of the hereafter and strive for it accordingly." This saying may seem to contradict the previous one, for if you balance the time you will spend in this world against the time you will spend in the hereafter, it will be nothing. Each of our Prophet's sayings is perfect; therefore, for those who would abandon their worldly duties, he has urged them to oppose this tendency by thinking of this world as eternal, so that they may give value to their duties. And for those who would pursue this world exclusively, the second measure: the time spent here against the time there, so that they may seek what is in fact eternal.

Sayyidina Ali related from the wisdom he gained from the Prophet, that exaggeration on the one had, and the total abandonment, on the other, of any aspect of life is a sign of ignorance. Therefore, in this matter of balance between different aspects of effort we have been urged to seek equilibrium. And our Naqshbandi predecessors recommend the following division of our day: eight hours for prayer and devotions and eight hours for seeking our sustenance, (and time devoted to our families may be considered as devotion, as Allah has ordered us to attend to them). Following such guidelines, even people with heavy responsibilities may find time for both work and prayer, like King Solomon and Sultan Abdul Hamid.

Question: What shall I do in my work situation where I am surrounded by people who are really devils, and are always trying to drag me down to their level? Shall I be very short with them, reject their familiarity and just go about my business?

Shaykh Nazim: There is no wisdom in pointing out people's faults to them directly, nor in behaving in such a way that your disapproval becomes very obvious. All you may do is to make some very generalized statements at an appropriate time without coming too close to directly attacking their actions or ideas, for there is nothing that the ego hates more than being blamed or accused.

All souls have wings, but the wings of sinners are broken, and they cannot fly until their wings heal, and that takes time. Meanwhile, they do not seek nests in high places – on roofs, mountains or trees – but crawl into the basement. Because they are imprisoned by their egos they remain in that dark surrounding, never seeing the light of day, only knowing artificial light.

They may in time emerge from that dark basement, but if you make them angry with you they will become even more stubborn. Allah Almighty warned the holy Prophet of the consequences of such an attitude when He said:

"And if you were short tempered, severe and hard hearted they would flee from you."

This verse indicates that only through exemplary tolerance and kindness can any impression be made on ill mannered and badly educated people.

It is not Allah Almighty's way to punish people, not even tyrants, until a divine messenger has been sent to them, to offer them a better way than the way of tyranny on which they tread. The door to repentance and just dealing is open to everyone, and it was the duty of the prophets and their inheritors to beckon all towards that door; all the more so the tyrants, as their bad actions may adversely affect millions of people or the whole world!

The very word "Pharaoh" has become synonymous with "tyrant." Our Lord teaches us the proper way of trying to turn a tyrant away from his tyranny, when He ordered Moses and Aaron, peace be upon them to:

"Go unto Pharaoh and speak to him smoothly and politely, that perhaps he may be guided."

Only later, when Pharaoh's intransigence became apparent, was Moses ordered to threaten him with divine wrath and to bring down divine retribution upon Pharaoh's people.

According to this divine wisdom, it is wrong for a believer to confront anyone with bad manners and derision. We have not been ordered to be quarrelsome and scowling, cursing and swearing people.

Whenever our grandshaykh would receive government officials, secret police or people who had come to his assembly to try and find fault, in order to oppose him, he, of course, could easily read their secret intentions. He always treated such people with special kindness, showing them extraordinary respect and deference. The result was that they would feel ashamed of their previous insincere intentions and go away with a good feeling about Grandshaykh, resolving to treat him respectfully from then on. Our grandshaykh's wife used to warn us: "If you see Grandshaykh making a great fuss over a visitor, beware of that person!"

Male and Female in Unity Oceans

There are so many books in this shop that I get drunk just looking at them, and these are just books on esoteric topics – we won't even begin to talk about the vastness of human knowledge that increases by leaps and bounds every day. The subject dealt with by the books in this shop can be called the "essence of knowledge" – wisdom. Knowledge may be arrived at through the process of experimentation and observation: it is the understanding of the observable. Knowledge is the fruit of thought, but wisdom is a grant from the Divine Presence imparted through contact with saints: wisdom imparts unto one the power to traverse the seven levels of heavenly knowledge.

Even if you were to read all the books in this shop, don't imagine that you would progress even one step towards those heavenly stations. No, all that will happen to the reader of all the books in this shop is that he will become fed up with esoteric subjects – like me – I have read too many books, and now I am fed up and can't even look at books. The key is only found in meeting a person who may impart wisdom to you, may help you arrive at your private station in the Divine Presence. Without the help of a guide you may catch a glimpse of something spiritual, then turn your back on it – like someone who goes to the movies, sees the show and then goes back to where he came from.

Book knowledge often merely serves to make people proud. We seek the sort of knowledge that may serve to make us humble, as proud people will eventually be debased and humble people elevated spiritually. Proud people are banished from the Divine Presence, whereas humble people are invited. Satan was puffed up with pride in his knowledge, and was exiled from the Divine Presence, but Adam humbled himself and was drawn near. Therefore, we have devoted our efforts to seeking knowledge of the heart, knowledge which serves us as a means for arriving at our destinations

The approach of our arrival will be signaled by a profound inner peace – as the soul loves to swim in that deep ocean of divine knowledge, just as a ship is partial to deep water. Your minds have limits but not your hearts, for they are receptacles of endless capacity; but you must open your hearts to this knowledge, as nothing may pass through what is closed.

Allah loves the brokenhearted. You are coveting a little water in a clay jug, but when you break it that water rejoins the lake from whence it came. Our egos try to prevent that reunion, and always object to any suggestion of the need to seek reunion. The main purpose of spiritual exercises in any tradition, East or West, is to enable us to overcome the objections put forward by our egos, so that we may pursue our journey to Unity Oceans.

The ego objects to losing its individuality in Unity Oceans, but the urge to pursue that quest is planted deeply within our nature; indeed, it is the compelling force behind the greatest of the ego's drives – sexuality. Sexuality is the expression of the need to attain unity. A man feels the need to unite with a woman, and vice versa, bodily and emotionally, and what a strong urge this is! But even this is only a reflection of the drive to attain unity with the divine, a reflection easily observable by every human being, whereas observation of the origin of this urge is comprehensible only to the elect. Allah Almighty created the two sexes with this overpowering need for each other, and made it impossible for one to feel whole without the presence of the other. Indeed the very physical structure of males and females is a sign that each must seek unity – and all of our souls, be we male or female, are seeking to merge with the Unity Oceans of Allah. It is that attraction that makes people so intent upon the opposite sex, though perhaps they don't understand it in such a way.

It is from that burning need for the divine that our friend here has retreated from worldly life. He is trying to break that jug and attain the endless beauty of that unity. All the beauty contained in nature – people, animals, plants and minerals – is not even a drop in the Ocean of that absolute beauty. The galaxies are swimming in His Power Oceans. Oh man, your soul is an endless source of secrets that no one can fathom but the Creator. What does it all mean? It means that all the sources gushing from your heart are streaming towards divine oceans.

At a Mountain Retreat

Question: Since our arrival at this retreat I have been pondering on the fact that in all spiritual traditions throughout the world and along the course of history, seekers of truth have sought solitude high up in mountain ranges, thus removing themselves from the society of men. Why is this necessary?

Shaykh Nazim: Mountains are closer to the sky – so if anything is sent down we may catch it first! Those people are waiting down by the lake to get it, but the one who climbs the mountain will surely intercept it!

Now all of you have retreated to this mountain, and though the surroundings are beautiful, no doubt, none of you have come here for a picnic; your intentions are more serious than that. We know what your secret intentions are in coming here, even if you, yourselves, are perhaps unable to clearly know or express what your purposes are. We know that only your hearts' yearning for their heavenly destinations has brought you here.

We must try to understand that we are pursuing a goal, and ascertain the direction of that goal and the reasons for our undertaking the journey. Then we must discover the best route leading to that goal. If a person wants to travel to Bern, for example, but just sets off on any road in any direction, he is surely wasting his effort.

We are all pursuing our individual courses, but we are fortunate to have gathered on this huge mountain, for it is a sign that your sense of purpose is strong, that the longing in your hearts is appearing through active endeavor towards your goals.

You have come here to receive light. If you felt yourselves to be bathing inwardly in light, what need would there have been for you to come here? Once Moses was traveling at night, when in the distance he saw a burning bush. He said to his wife: "Behold, a fire in the distance! I will go ahead and gather some embers, that we may have light and warm ourselves thereby." Moses was attracted to that burning bush – and, unwittingly, to a meeting with his Lord – because he was in cold and dark surroundings, and thus he was in need of seeking warmth and light. If they had already been basking in the warmth of a campfire, he would never have pursued embers.

Similarly, he who feels himself in need of light comes to such a mountain retreat as this. But, just as Moses intended to get embers and bring them to his family that they might benefit from the warmth and light, so must we take a light from here to our people to banish darkness from their hearts. This is our goal, but firstly, we must also banish coldness from our hearts, and from between them, as in our times there is a terrible frigidity between the hearts of people, creeping out from the coldness of their individual hearts.

So, it is important that when you retreat to such a refuge as this, you are not totally alone, but with fellow seekers from every part of Europe, and thereby have an opportunity to train yourselves with each other, so that you may return to your respective communities capable of generating warmth of heart to those people as well, to take what you have received on the mountain down with you to the valley, and share it with even one of those people to whom climbing a mountain might never occur.

There is no benefit in any of you remaining here indefinitely; rather you may derive full benefit from being here between three and forty days. Forty days is the term of completion, now and through the course of history. Therefore, many of the prophets, among them one of the highest ranking of the prophets, Moses, have been ordered to retreat for forty days. Moses was ordered to be alone on Mount Sinai for that term, and after the completion of that term he was granted divine light and given commandments to be transmitted to his people, as well as a mission of truth to Pharaoh and his people.

Light your candle here, and then light others' candles. You must be ambassadors of light, goodness and contentment in God. In this way you may fulfill your true purpose – God's purpose for your lives – and reach your destinations, otherwise you may lose yourself like a wanderer in a vast desert with no compass and no map. Keep these words with you wherever you go and they should show you your way.

Moses received light, wisdom and guidance, then the Lord ordered him to, "Go unto Pharaoh and the Egyptians. Give this light to him and to his nation, to bring them out of darkness." And the Virgin Mary brought Jesus into the world and cared for him until he was ready to give his light to his people – she never tried to keep him for herself. You must also be for others: that is the best and highest of ways. He who is only for himself is greedy.

We must try to be for others more than for ourselves. It is acceptable if we live for ourselves as well as for others, but it is the lowest acceptable level. To sacrifice ourselves for others is the highest level, the level of all the prophets.

If not for our egos, such self sacrifice would be easy, we would all be angelic; but as we are all in the possession of our egos rather than being the possessors of our egos, we need to come here to train ourselves in the way of fighting the ego. Don't underestimate the scale of that battle, for indeed, fighting a whole nation single handedly is an easier task. Your determination to really strive for such a goal will certainly be tested, and it is a good sign that you have come to such a place as this. But if you try to stay here, to declare all out war on the ego, the ego will defeat you. Your egos have thousands of tricks and traps, therefore, it is too dangerous to try to fight it continuously   no, you must struggle, then rest. Even soldiers in the front lines must sleep and also be relieved or they will become exhausted and easily overcome.

Now, it is not important that I give you spiritual exercises to practice during your retreat. If I do, they may be difficult for you to practice. We have other ways of transmitting spiritual power from heart to heart, and as long as I am permitted to be here, not a moment will be devoid of its effect. We have been authorized by Grand Masters, and he who stands under their umbrella reaches his destination safely.

Allah's Dye: Essence and Attributes

Question: Of the theories of Sigmund Freud many have by now been disproven and discarded, but through my experience as a psychiatrist I have come to believe that at least one basic theory is true: that, based upon our experience as a child, and based upon our connection to our parents, we internalize these experiences and later tend to see everything in the world in that perspective. For example, if a child has been beaten excessively by his father, he grows up seeing everything around him as potentially dangerous, so he is always living in fear that people may "strike" him as his father did. On the other hand, someone who had an overindulgent, loving mother may be predisposed to seeing the world at large as loving and indulgent, and therefore may have problems facing up to the realities of adulthood. I have confirmed these theories in my own work, and as far as I can tell they bear out in reality on the psychological, not necessarily the spiritual level.

Shaykh Nazim: While it is true that the effects of one's childhood environment may leave their imprint on the adult personality, the inborn personality is stronger still. A rose may be planted in London or in Cyprus, and it may grow in either place. If it grows in London, it will, as a result of the cold and wet climate, remain fresh over a long period of time, but will not be fragrant. If it grows in Cyprus, on the other hand, because of the hot and dry climate it will only remain fresh for a short period of time, but will be very fragrant while it lasts. Whatever the characteristics of its life, a rose is a rose, in London or in Cyprus, and never will it be jasmine or lilac.

The point is that the Creator has given each person a unique and distinct personality. Even identical twins have unmistakably different personalities, so I am not referring to "heredity" (as identical twins are genetically identical). I am not promoting the effects of "heredity" over those of "environment", but am referring to another factor, a spiritual one, beyond the scope of psychological debate. Our grandshaykh explained that each personality is an emanation of a divine Name, a unique attribute of God, and that there are as many divine attributes as there are human beings – and more, endlessly. Therefore, on the purest spiritual level, each and every individual is a unique manifestation of God.

In the Quranic rendering of the story of the Last Supper, the twelve apostles asked Jesus: *"Is your Lord able to cause a supper to descend to us from heaven?"*

Notice that they did not ask if "our Lord" or "the Lord" could cause the manifestation of this miracle, but whether "your Lord" could. Don't let this wording lead you to believe that the apostles were skeptics regarding the existence of God, and therefore said "your Lord" rather than "our Lord" or "the Lord." No, their belief in the existence of God was unshakable. They said "your Lord" because the performance of this miracle was directly related to the attributes of God manifest in and through Jesus Christ, the attributes that enabled him to manifest so many miracles.

In the same way that the divine manifested through Jesus in just that way, so does the divine manifest through each and every personality – that is the essence of each soul, and it is not subject to change. But just as the beauty of a diamond may be enhanced by a beautiful gold ring or be hidden by wrapping it in cotton, so do external influences determine to what extent that divine personality is able to shine forth.

Question: Psychoanalysis claims that problems stem from the personality, but you are saying that the personality is beyond these influences, and that only some superficial conditioning causes behavior abnormalities.

Shaykh Nazim: The divinely ordained personality is always sound and intact, but as, for example, a consistently strong wind may cause a tree to grow crooked so one's environment can affect one's development. We must draw a distinction between "essence" and "attribute." There is an essence to everything. You are tall, for example, but without a body "tall" is a meaningless adjective. Similarly, "good" and "bad" manifestations are impossible without a person to manifest them. It is only the adjectives that are influenced by the atmosphere. One hundred years ago there was a religiously observant atmosphere in this country, now there is an atheist atmosphere, and the manifestations of this atmosphere can only be altered with the greatest difficulty.

Question: For example, a man may be raised in a quarrelsome surrounding, and thus he grows up fearful. You may encourage him to leave the situation he is in, but by now he has internalized this quarrelsomeness and carries it with him. What can be done to help such a person?

Shaykh Nazim: It is for this reason that children must be brought up properly, in a way that imparts good characteristics to them. Of course this is only possible if we possess these good characteristics ourselves. According to the holy Prophet, newborn babies are all born in perfect harmony with their Lord's will – it is only the parents who influence them to oppose His will. Despite this, the essence is ever the same manifestation of divine perfection – like indelible ink that can be covered but never removed. In the end, all of those coats of cheap paint will flake off and there will remain only the original unfaded color. This is what is referred to in the holy Quran as "Allah's dye."

You may use your position as a psychiatrist in order to apply "paint remover." You are obliged, however, to quickly apply another layer, but a more acceptable one. Unfortunately, most psychiatrists have no "paint remover" all, and are only applying the new coat over the old one. Thus they estrange their patients even more from that original divine coat, so that in the end there is even more to remove.

Question: What method can I apply as a "paint remover"? If I mention to people anything even remotely related to religion they get angry and stop listening.

Shaykh Nazim: You must locate the open door. People have an allergy against religion, so don't mention it. We have ninety nine methods to be utilized in the treatment of disturbed people, so when you have incorporated enough of this teaching you will receive inspiration that will guide you to the application of suitable methods. In the meantime you must keep a journal in which you record the details of your patients' afflictions, and analyze their personalities.

Question: Now I'm going to be a little more difficult. One notices many personality disorders among your disciples – myself included – we needn't talk only of mental patients. Despite the practices we follow and the conscious attempts we make to improve ourselves, the character disorders seem to persist. I am not saying that there is no improvement or progress, but it can be observed that many of the problems are still there, even in some cases after many years.

Shaykh Nazim: No psychiatrist can ever encounter as much resistance to the treatment he is giving his patients as we encounter in our training of Sufi aspirants. The ego is allergic to "paint remover"; that is why you, in your position, can only hope to remove a particularly unsatisfactory layer and quickly replace it with another. My job is one that encounters serious and terrible resistance from the ego, as I am trying to remove all the paint and lay bare the original "dye of Allah" which pertains to the divine essence, the original spiritual personality. But the ego wants only that its layers of paint are never removed. Even when people come to see a Sufi shaykh their egos are hoping to obtain more adornments, but it is our duty to take everything from the hands of the ego, not to adorn it further: to undermine its possessiveness and dissipate acquired characteristics in favor of original ones.

Therefore, when people first come I try to give them something, but when I leave I collect it from them. If I were to say this to you at first and immediately set to removing the layers of ego, quickly you would all escape from my hands and I would finally be able to retire. To move a mountain is an easier task than removing one of the acquired characteristics of our egos. Our egos are but vehicles to make possible for our souls to exist in this realm, but the ego puts forward claims to being the man and not just the horse. Our job is to make this all clear and to help people get their horses under control. If this task were easy, all religious scholars would be shaykhs and all shaykhs would be Grand Masters. But the ego is so difficult to tackle that we can never find such facility in reaching high stations – quite to the contrary. We find most aspirants bogged down at their present levels and sinking.

As for psychiatrists, only a few of them understand the nature of personality and how to go about changing it. Most of them add only more to the already heavy burden of their customers – this you know better than I. They cannot affect the soul with their methods; at best they can train the horse to behave a little more obediently. In order to affect the rider of the horse there must be a murshid (master or guide) at work. A real murshid must know what to do for his patients, or else he is not a guide. If a doctor doesn't know how to treat his patients' illnesses he is useless. He may have read so many medical books, but if he doesn't know what to do when a sick person comes to him he is useless.

Question: You say that every person is guided by one attribute of Allah. If a person learns this attribute does it serve as a guideline for him in his quest to reach his goal?

Shaykh Nazim: Yes, and it is important to know it, but it is a difficult burden of knowledge to carry now. It is of utmost importance that you first arrive to the point of controlling your horses, or you may attack people with the power you have gained. Who in their right mind would grant me permission to drive a truck or a bus? I would only leave a trail of wreckage in my wake. I can't even control a small car, so what about those huge vehicles? Therefore, a murshid will never impart any glimpse of the realities of the individual divine names without having first established that aspirant in the control of his horse.

Question: What happens if a person dies without these layers of ego having been removed?

Shaykh Nazim: That original dye must still appear. That person may appear to you to be under the influence of illusion, but at the time of death Allah is pursuing His Claims on His servants, and though Satan may fight for him, Allah is always victorious. He says: "Oh Satan, even though this person may have followed you in his actions, the essence which I granted him has been preserved intact." These are the secrets of destiny, and no one can speak of them.

Question: What about people who refuse to accept a guide?

Shaykh Nazim: Their horses are very strong and wild. If you approach them from the front they will bite you, if from the back they will kick.

Question: When I organize seminars for people, I realize that they have a great deal of resistance to this kind of approach, to fighting the ego, rather they want to have access to miraculous powers and insights: to travel astrally, read people's minds, and they want to gain these powers by any means – except fighting the ego.

Shaykh Nazim: Everyone wants to become a doctor or engineer without the trouble of going to a university and struggling through long and arduous studies. They all want to buy instant diplomas: but what validity do they have? If I were to go to your country and claim that I was an expert on anything, even psychiatry, they would say to me, "Where are you coming from, the moon?" Yes, people are foolish. They want to achieve everything without effort, to take everything without stretching out their hands. It is not easy to receive spiritual authority.

Question: Allah Almighty has created distinctions between people. Do these apparent distinctions relate only to the attributes of their egos or also to their spiritual essences?

Shaykh Nazim: Just as there are endless stars in the sky, each having distinct characteristics, so do people's inner realities differ. If the inner realities of even one person were to be completely unveiled, the stars and the whole universe would vanish, so don't think that we are just caricatures. The essential reality of each soul is an unchanging reality in the Divine Presence, but Allah Almighty has created so many different kinds of people to benefit each other through their interaction, to mutually reveal divine attributes. We can say that, for as many of the children of Adam as appear in existence, there are as many distinct divine attributes; but that is only an approximation, for the reality cannot be explained through words nor to the mind.

Until we are able to rise above the level of the mind, people themselves serve as the means of attaining a state of preparedness for spiritual life, and our various conflicts and "scrapes" serve as a means of polishing the heart.

Once, in the market of Damascus, I observed a blacksmith polishing some chains. How did he do it? The middle part of the chain was wrapped in a skin, while four, six or eight people pulled each end back and forth. Through this scraping together the chains were polished. We must be open to the wisdom around us.

Some Questions of an Expatriate Muslim

Question: One of the points that draws Westerners to Islam is the spirit of universal religion contained in it, the ideal of one nation, of a brotherhood that potentially encompasses all of mankind, every kind and color. In practice however, one still finds oneself relating more closely to people of one's own cultural or ethnic background, than to those whose background is similar in some respects, and only distantly to people whose life experiences have been totally different.

Shaykh Nazim: How shall Westerners, people who have lived the much sought after life and have sought after something better, feel much affinity with people who are obsessed only with that way of life you already found lacking? When you tell them your experiences you should feel only frustrated and as if you are talking to the wall. For them you are strange and threatening, it is as if you were ridiculing them and their aspirations. They may feel especially bewildered when you appear in the comfortable native clothes of their native lands, when they are very proud to have finally become "civilized." It is necessary for them to think of you as some sort of Afghani mountaineers or Egyptian peasants.

It is natural for people of different cultures to be intrigued by certain aspects of other cultures, even if it only manifests itself in eating the food of that country from time to time in a restaurant. Still, there must be that attraction, and it is pleasing to Allah, as He said:

"I have made you to be of different colors and languages that you may come to know each other, and to understand that the best of you is only the one who honors his Lord."

It is also only natural that there should be some element of confusion in the attempts by people of one culture to understand those of another.

It is not surprising that we should incline towards those things that are familiar to us from childhood, and towards people who share those experiences. Don't let that disturb you, as in reality it is a reflection of our longing for our original spiritual homeland, for as the holy Prophet said, *"Love of one's homeland is of faith."*

Question: I have been living in Muslim countries for a long time, but still I don't feel entirely at home there, nor any longer, in the land of my birth.

Shaykh Nazim: We shall send you to the moon. Feeling that one is neither Occidental nor Oriental is a sign of real faith, as the holy Quran declares that divine lights are neither Oriental nor Occidental. Your goal must be to belong to your Lord, not to East or to West. Identification with one's worldly homeland and with all that pertains to it is a reflection of the soul's longing for its heavenly homeland; but we must remember that it is only a reflection and not the original. Until we have love for our original homeland we will hate the very thought of death, shrink from our reunion with our Lord, and that is very dangerous. Therefore, we are seeking a way to increase our faith to the level where we will be burning to meet Him, and we must know that He will be pleased to receive us.

The Breakdown of the Family

Question: One of the most alarming developments in modern society is the breakdown of the family. First, the extended family ceased to exert its previous influence on people, and the nuclear family became the primary identification for individuals. Subsequently, the nuclear family has proved to be built on shaky foundations. Nowadays, so many children grow up with only one parent, and old people are relegated to old age homes. What is happening to mankind?

Shaykh Nazim: All these are symptoms of the disease. The tree of humanity has been stricken with the blight of atheism. I am not referring to a blight that has afflicted a branch or two, but to one that has rotted all the branches to the core. Therefore, what is ultimately called for is a drastic cutting back of that tree, so that new, healthy and strong branches may emerge from the trunk. But, as it is not in our power to apply any general measures we must be content with the role of one who digs a well in the middle of a barren wilderness, and thereby extracts enough water to make a few trees bloom. It is not in our hands to alter the general condition of mankind, but when that power, the power of the Divine Presence is released, an empowered envoy will come to prune back the diseased branches.

Question: Under these circumstances, what can we do in order to raise our children to become aware, openhearted and conscientious believers?

Shaykh Nazim: Once I went to visit the botanical gardens, Kew Gardens in London. There is a greenhouse with coconut palms, citrus trees and other tropical and sub tropical trees and plants in abundance, growing and thriving – but they were protected from the elements. The other trees were so big and proud, saying, "We are not in prison! We are free!" Each one of those huge trees is getting all that it needs from the northern European climate, but can any of them produce a mango or a coconut? Trees that do produce such exotic fruits in such an inimical climate cannot be left to grow outside of glass. We must understand the wisdom in this example. It is imperative that we imprison our children in a greenhouse, that lets them observe the outside world, but separates them from its cold blasts, that admits the beneficial rays of the sun and intensifies them, but keeps out the air pollution.

Your "prison" must be transparent. Your children must be aware of what goes on in the outside world. That transparency allows for the passage of a kind of inoculation against the diseases of the polluted surroundings. Whoever has no anti bodies must perish. If the outside world is allowed to gather too much of an aura of mystery, it will seem all the more attractive and they will be all the more vulnerable. In this manner we must seek a middle way in raising our children. Sayyidina Ali once said: "The ways of extremism are the ways of ignorance." In order to avoid one extreme I have been discouraging our sons and daughters and seekers of truth in general, from establishing communities entirely separate from the community at large. There is a proverb: "Everything prohibited is especially attractive." You may be mature and developed people who have chosen this way of life, but your children have not, as of yet chosen, and ultimately they must choose, as we are not residing on the moon, established there as a single community with one lifestyle. No, they must know that this is a wide world comprising various people and races, abounding in religions and lifestyles.

Even if you were to immigrate to a Muslim country, your children would be curious about the land of your origin, and about their relatives there. It is important that you take them and bring them into contact with their grandparents, aunts, uncles and other relations, even if you seem to have very little in common with them.

You must also take your children, from time to time, to the big cities. At first they may find the hustle and bustle exciting, but quickly they will catch "cold", and on their own arrive at a perception of the special atmosphere, the warmth and blessedness found only in the homes of believers, and will be able to contrast it with the wildness of the city streets. If they are kept from those cities long enough and only experience them during or after puberty – watch out! So don't neglect to give your children their "vaccinations", and if you see them developing bad traits you may gently nudge them in the right direction.

God is Our Guarantor

We pray to our Lord to lift the heaviness off our hearts: and no one can lift those burdens except He Alone. Nowadays, huge industries have been built up whose only function is to provide diversion and amusement for people. Indeed, most industry falls under this category: the product that sells is not simply the one that fulfills a need, but the one that diverts people from the awareness of their misery – thus television, videos, sports cars, fashions, and games are the new necessities of life.

All of these products of diversion have to compete with each other to gain their portion of the market, thus, another huge industry: advertising. So, as we drive through the streets, beautiful people with clean white smiles come to meet us from their billboards and testify that, if only we buy such and such a product, we will look as good as they do, and always be surrounded by other beautiful people. The same is true of television ads: all are happy and laughing people.

But he to whom Allah Almighty has granted penetrating vision may observe that these people are smiling the "smile of the skeleton", the smile which always appears on skulls: all is just show, inside they are empty. This is a strange glimpse of reality that has been shown to me many times: what people call pleasure is only a kind of forced enjoyment.

Very young people may perhaps really feel enjoyment, as everything new is tasteful, but as they continue on this way, more and more they feel boredom setting in, that pleasure becoming but a routine. As a result they go further and further on the same way, to see if they can outreach the shadow of routine that makes all pleasures tasteless. Though they cannot win this race, they keep on running, progressing towards extremes of stimulation, but still feeling no pleasure. This disappointment and the consequent misery result from the mistaken assumption that "more is better." For example, a spoonful of honey is sweeter than a cupful which will only make you sick. But because the philosophy of endless greed is now the common creed, people think that finding a beehive would be their greatest good fortune. How wrong they are!

Oh people who claim to possess understanding, you must understand that your Lord has placed a hindrance before the fulfillment of some of your desires only for your own good, not because He enjoys depriving you of something good. If something is prohibited by religion it is only because that so called pleasure is a trap to catch you into suffering. But nowadays no one accepts this reality, or even if one does accept, or is attracted to any religion, seeks to ignore moral codes, because he has been taught that exercising absolute freedom is the only way to fulfillment. This is the doctrine that is burning people's faith, and it is in conflict with all world religions, East and West; but onward they march, with grimaces that are supposed to be smiles. They pretend to taste, but taste nothing, because you can't enjoy eating unless you are hungry, can't enjoy drinking unless you are thirsty. Their way is the way of the total destruction of their physical bodies and their spiritual lives.

Later in the day I saw something else that deeply affected my heart. As I looked outside I saw some sparrows hopping about on the roof. We also have sparrows in Cyprus, and I wondered what the living conditions were like for sparrows here in London. So I asked the sparrow: "Are you in any difficulties living here in London? If so, I may ask the sparrows in Cyprus to send you some aid." It replied: "Thank you, but we are all satisfied and we are not in need of any assistance at all. It doesn't matter to us that we are living in such an expensive country – even in Moscow our kind are alright. We are happy and free, never caught up in any crisis. Our salaries are sufficient and always paid on time, and it is all the same to us whether we live in Hampstead or Brixton, East End or Buckingham Palace: we receive our sustenance and glorify our Lord, saying, 'Allah, Allah'. If you can be more like us you may be happy – no suffering, no hospitals, no prisons, no passports – we are traveling freely from country to country, and we require no expensive insurance policies, our Lord is our guarantor. Oh Son of Adam, you must be more like us, then you will be happy, and have no need to fight and quarrel." Then he flew away.

Look, those sparrows are pleased with their Lord, and Allah is pleased with those who are pleased with Him. Therefore, you must seek ways to make Allah pleased with you. We walk this earth with a heavy burden of ego, and of course it is impossible for us to be so light, to flutter and twitter without a care in the world like sparrows, but we can emulate their ways in the trust of God. He Almighty is the Only One who can guarantee your future: you cannot determine what will happen to you, and you cannot know what accidents or misfortunes may befall you, your spouse, your children, nation or business. Don't put your trust in your job, your power, your knowledge or your beauty, for it may be that none of this will avail you when you are the must vulnerable. This is an undeniable fact, and somewhere within themselves people know this. Therefore, those skeleton smiles, when dropped, revert to the frowns that reflect how the people are really feeling.

But the prophets and the Friends of God have received a guarantee from their Lord, a guarantee of protection and care: and according to the level of your faith you too may attain a guarantee of protection and care, and the serenity that results from such assurance.

The shadow of worry pursues the "uninsured", and just as an aspirin may temporarily alleviate the symptoms o a migraine headache, but not cure its causes, so do temporary pleasures make people temporarily oblivious of their miseries. The guarantee of our Lord gives us permanent pleasure, and its source is in our hearts. Whoever has such a fountain in his heart need not be a consumer in the amusement market. Why should he need to escape from his house every night to the discotheque, theater or gambling casino when his heart provides him with all he needs to be happy?

We must aspire to take the keys to our inner treasures, lest all we achieve in our lives is to make ourselves "stimulation addicts"; and ultimately, we must carry responsibility for wasting our lives in such a manner. Those enjoyments are only pain killers, and you may live for a while on a diet of pain killers if you wish, but ultimately they will kill you.

Why Depression?

Why are people afflicted with depression? No, sexual relations are not the primary cause of depression – there are other factors, and when these factors are present everything in life feels like a punishment and ceases to function normally, even sex which is normally the most enjoyable of activities. When normal relationships are disrupted by the presence of the root causes of depression, sex partners can only be a means for mutual punishment: each one "takes", then escapes from the other – into depression.

The main cause of depression is the effect of memory upon people. Most people harbor in themselves some very deep regrets about their own past actions or about what they feel to be wrong decisions or mistakes made through the course of their lives. When we recall such painful events, a fire roars out of control through our hearts. Then we arrive at a gaping hole in our hearts that cannot be filled, no matter what we try to fill it with – so deep are our regrets.

Our present life becomes a bridge between the past and future, between two terrible visions: haunting memories and anxiety filled anticipation of the future. Worrying about our future makes us crazy, and all that modern medical science can do about it is to offer people some dangerous drugs specially designed to cloud both memory and anticipation. These are terrible and dangerous methods, for when people regain their wits, their despair will become even more acute. Allah in His wisdom created brain cells non renewable. Those dangerous drugs kill brain cells, and once they are killed they are never replaced.

Since it is impossible to change the past, we must be patient in the face of painful memories and no one can attain such patience without being a believer – and not just a believer in name, but also a person of deep faith. Those memories will persist as memories, but faith may effectively neutralize their painful effects. He who has been absorbed in the love of God may feel himself to have made a new beginning and to have left painful memories far behind.

There is a tradition of the holy Prophet: "Of actions, only the final one counts." We must know that the only step of real importance in our lives is the last step – was it on the right way or on the path of iniquity? So many saints have once been big sinners, and every mistake we make is an opportunity to realize something valuable about ourselves, and to awaken to the need for improvement. The past had best be left behind us. It is a completed chapter, and there is no need to harp upon it. What is important is to consider where you are headed. Even though you may be nearing the end of your life, don't be discouraged if it seems to have been spent frivolously – just make your last step count.

Another cause of depression is hopelessness. We, as servants of a great God, have no right to be hopeless – no. The Lord may change everything in a second – everything. He whose faith is strong will never doubt that his Lord ultimately intends good for him in this life and the next, and he will be patient through adversity, looking for the Lord's promised respite. As for unbelievers, abysmal despair follows on the heels of worldly ambition, as all their hopes are dashed on the rocks of time. But the heart of the believer is a vessel that sails safely through such danger, with the Lord as his guide, and his faith in the guide keeps his heart afloat through stormy seas, until at last the goal is attained – endless Mercy Oceans. I know that my bad actions are a hindrance between my Lord and myself, but I believe that His Mercy Oceans will engulf my heart and that I will be freed of my bad attributes, and be granted a new personality, suitable for Mercy Oceans.

Allah is With the Patient

Whenever we direct our hearts towards our Lord Almighty we are immersed in inner peace, and when we turn away from Him we are stranded at the bottom of a deep and dark well seething with snakes, scorpions and spiders.

Grandshaykh told me a story of a man who always felt aggravated by his surroundings who always felt as if people were disturbing his peace of mind. One day he got so fed up with the society of men that he decided to leave it behind and become a cave dwelling hermit. So he settled all of his affairs and retired to a remote mountainside. After searching for many days he finally found a cave suitable for his purposes, and occupied it, saying: "There is no one here and no one knows where I am. I am finally in peace."

Just as he was saying this to himself, someone passed in the valley below, looked up at the mountainside and noticed a very beautiful rock just near that cave. "I must have a piece of that colorful rock," he said to himself, and began hacking away at it: tak! tak! tak!

At this the man in the cave became really exasperated and said: "Oh my Lord, I try to escape from people and You send me this! There are so many mountains, why did You have to send him to this one?"

No one can escape discomfort in this life, as the holy Prophet said, *"There is no rest in this world."* You may live in a city or a village, even on the side of a mountain – but all you will discover is that this life is made of unrest. We have been ordered to be patient in the face of this situation, for, "He who is patient ultimately succeeds." Allah sends us trials and burdens in accordance with our capacities, but every single person must carry some burden through this life. We will be asked to carry burdens in accordance with our faith power. In our times believers will be loaded to their absolute capacities, as spiritually blind people have made sure to make the lives of believers as difficult as possible.

The Conversion of the Magicians

Allah Almighty rewards people according to their intentions. If a person is sincere and has good intentions he will be rewarded by his Lord, no matter what his religion may be. Don't hold your Lord's mercy to be any less than this.

I once heard a tale about a Zoroastrian living in Baghdad in the time of the Abbasid Khaliphs. After his death a grandshaykh saw him in a dream amidst the joys of paradise. That shaykh was surprised and said to him: "How is it that you are in paradise when you spent your life worshipping fire?" He replied: "Oh my Lord's servant, there is only one reason for my being here in paradise. It is on account of one very simple action that I never took any notice of – after it happened I forgot about it completely, and certainly I never expected to be rewarded eternally for it, but so has it come to pass." When Allah Almighty wants to find a way to redeem His creatures, surely He will find that way. He continued: "One day during the fasting month of Ramadan, my young son was sitting in front of the house eating a piece of bread. I pulled his ear and scolded him saying, 'May no one else ever pull your ear like this, here or hereafter! This is a holy month for the Muslims, they are fasting, so how can you show such blatant disrespect for their customs?' Allah was pleased with me for my respect of His holy month, and my respect for the feelings of my neighbors, and so here I am."

That man was a Zoroastrian and cannot be expected to have fasted in Ramadan: that is not his responsibility, he was not Muslim. Secondly, the son was only a small boy, and small children are not required to fast in any case. But even though he may not have participated in the fast, he respected it and taught his young son to do the same.

Let me give you another example of the value of showing respect to all that pertains to God and his beloved people: when Moses agreed to a showdown with the magicians. Pharaoh assembled 250,000 wizards to overwhelm Moses with their magical powers. They all arrived at the plain where the competition was to be held, decked out in such terrifying costumes that anyone would have been overcome with fear just looking at their numbers and forms. From the opposite direction Moses approached in his simple pastoral outfit, staff in hand. Then the chief magician stepped forward and Moses stood firmly in front of him. Moses looked at him intensely – divine light penetrated the heart of the wizard, and it melted. He asked Moses humbly: "Will you cast your magic first or shall we be the first to cast?" His respectful addressing of Moses in this manner was a sign that faith had entered his heart. In fact, he had started to receive inspiration when he first saw Moses approach, facing such a fearsome horde alone and unperturbed. It was then that he knew that Moses must be a messenger of God, for who else could be so fearless? Once he understood that Moses was not representing himself, but was a divine messenger, he lowered the wing of humility, and this caused the Lord to be pleased with the whole group of magicians, even though the practice of magic is strongly forbidden by divine Commandment.

When Moses told them to go ahead and manifest whatever they had prepared, the seed of faith had already begun to sprout in their hearts, and the miracle he performed only served to put a seal on their faith. They had cast their staffs, and each one had taken on the appearance of a terrible snake, so that even Moses himself wondered at such a show. But when Moses threw his staff, Allah caused a huge dragon to appear, a dragon that could swallow all the magicians had produced, a dragon whose mouth was a mile high and a mile wide. Then, when the dragon had devoured all of the snakes, it turned and asked, "Where is Pharaoh?" and turned towards the pavilion from which Pharaoh was witnessing the event, and it appeared to be ready to swallow the whole pavilion.

But it was not God's intention to kill Pharaoh then and there, but to give him a humbling lesson, that haply he might repent and turn towards truth. But the lesson imparted here involved a humbling much more basic and undeniable than the defeat of Pharaoh's magicians and their subsequent conversion to the true religion, a drastic change in Pharaoh's bowel habits that should have caused Pharaoh to reconsider his spurious claim to godhood. Prior to this event Pharaoh used to support his claim to divinity by the fact that he had hardly ever moved his bowels – only once in forty days. But from the time that the serpent turned and asked: "Where is Pharaoh?" Pharaoh had to move his bowels forty times a day, and thereby humble himself by entering the "house of health" more often than any of his nation.

Yes, Allah humbled him, but he accepted not the robe of humility. When the wizards saw the miracle that Moses had wrought they immediately threw themselves into humble prostration, and at that moment each of them beheld his place in paradise.

When Pharaoh emerged from the water closet to find that his magicians had turned from worshipping him to the worship of the One True God, he was furious. "What are you doing?! You were all in cahoots with Moses from the beginning. Now it is clear – he is your secret chief, the one who taught you all of your tricks. I shall cut off your hands and feet and crucify you on the trunks of palm trees! Then you will know who is powerful!" They replied: "Do what you will, but you can only torture our physical bodies. Our souls are free, for we now know that we belong to the Lord of the worlds."

From the stories of the conversion of the magicians and that of the Zoroastrian of Baghdad, we can realize the connection between good intentions towards the servants of God and respect of His commands, and the unveiling of deeply hidden faith. We must never lose hope that Allah's all embracing mercy will encompass us, and all His weak servants.

Is There No Escape?

Oh suffering people, you may attain peace only through the remembrance of your Lord. Nowadays most people feel themselves to be suffering, to be in misery, and the question most often asked is: "To where may I escape from my problems?" The coming of such times is predicted in all holy books, and finally, also, in the holy Quran, which describes suffering people who ask: "To where may we escape?" The portrayal of such times makes the hearts of believers shrink in horror, but as I look at the human beings of our time I see pain written on their faces and hear them shouting this very question. But no matter where you run, you are bound to find a mountain of troubles even more formidable than the one from which you have escaped.

Now people are all trying to escape from their situations. Orientals flee to the West in search of freedom and wealth, while Westerners flee from a sea of materialism to the Orient to find a traditional way of life. Peasants can no longer stand to live in the countryside and flee to cities seeking the "civilized" life, and city dwellers, ill with civilization's diseases flock to the countryside to seek a wholesome lifestyle. But so often, even when people manage to escape from one place to another, one culture to another, one climate to another or from one marriage to another, seeking relief from their miseries, they only find themselves faced with another set of miseries, and then they fall into disillusionment and hopelessness.

The present state of affairs is the fulfillment of the prophecy of the holy Prophet in which he predicted that there would come a time when people would pass through cemeteries and say: "If only we were among you, or if only you could be in our places and we in yours! You are at rest, but we are in torment; oh, how lucky you are to have lived in earlier times and never to have seen these days!"

So where is a shelter from these miseries to be found? Allah Almighty answers the question of those desperate people, saying: "Flee to your Lord!" The answer is very simple, but our egos rebel against our fleeing in that direction, saying: "No, I won't permit you to flee to anyone but me alone, nor to take another shelter than mine, because I have my own will, my own knowledge and my own ideals: they are all we need, so come into my shelter!" But verily the ego's shelter is full of leaks; it cannot keep out the downpour of tribulation!

Both the Torah and the Quran tell us the story of Noah, peace be upon him, and even now may we derive wisdom and a valuable lesson from the events that occurred during the life of that most ancient prophet. No event in history shows us more plainly how the only real shelter is with our Lord, and how the shelter created by our minds will be swept away. Noah was sent to his Nation and to all people living at his time. No prophet was ever granted such a miraculous lifespan – nine hundred and fifty years – but no prophet was ever afflicted with such persistent rejection and persecution either.

Whenever he would arise and exhort his people they would stone him until he was knocked unconscious. The story is well known. Finally, after centuries of vain attempts to guide the people, he prayed: "Oh my Lord, You must not leave on the face of the earth even one household of these hard hearted people, for no child is born to them except that he becomes an even greater tyrant than his parents. If You leave them be they will lead astray even those few people who have believed in You. Oh my Lord, spare and forgive me and my family and those believers who are with us."

Then the Lord granted his prayer and resolved to destroy the wicked by sending a flood to cover the earth, and He commanded Noah to build an ark as a shelter for the few believers and for a male and female of each kind of animal. Then Noah set out to build the Ark, not at the seaside, but in the midst of dry land. Some people asked him: "Oh Noah, what are you building?" "I am building an Ark as a shelter against a great flood that the Lord will send upon the earth." "Then why don't you build it by the sea instead of on this high ground, for even if it rains as you say it will, here there will only be wild torrents rushing to the sea, and you may have a rough ride down such a wild river", they said sarcastically. "No", Noah said, "this will be a flood like no other, a flood that will leave nothing high and dry, and no rivers rushing to the sea: when this rain falls all will be sea." They only laughed scornfully and went off saying: "Such an old, old man, and yet he preaches the same nonsense he always has, along with threats of a flood to scare us into his religion!"

And finally, when Noah had completed the construction of the Ark, he bade his family and all the believers to enter. All of them hastened aboard, except for one of his sons, who had been influenced by the logic of those who had ridiculed his father. He said. "I don't need to board that rickety vessel. If it really rains as you say, I will seek refuge on the top of a mountain. It never floods there, only in valleys. This is a clear natural law, and I trust my own perception and logic. I know where floods go and where they don't." Noah pleaded with him: "Oh my son, you think that you know, but you are wrong: come aboard and you will be safe!" But the son stubbornly held to his judgment, a judgment that would have been correct in the face of any other flood the world had ever known, save this one, which inundated the earth up to seventy yards above the peak Noah's son had climbed, and he perished.

In this tale is contained a lesson for all men who have placed their trust in the products of their own minds, and for their sake we are recounting the story of the fate of Noah's son when he took to the mountain instead of to the Ark. And in our times whole nations are seeking to escape from the ever rising level of the misery flood by adopting solutions that accord with their mental calculations, while not opposing their egos' dictates – they are climbing mountains instead of boarding the Ark. The proponents of such concocted solutions to the world's problems stand on mountaintops and call people to their own "high and dry" shelters. Each one calls out: "Come here! Climb this peak, not that one: ours is the safe peak!" But slowly, slowly their island peaks shrink in the face of the rising waters, and soon all will be submerged; to drown in the sea of misery is a terrible end.

But the key to redemption is repentance, and therefore, in the sight of Allah even the case of those who have run to the mountains instead of the Ark and have fallen into the sea is not hopeless, for Allah heard the prayer of Jonah from the belly of a whale: "Oh my Lord, there is no God beside You. Glorified be Your Name! Verily, I have been a wrongdoer!" He turned to his Lord completely, and Allah saved him from that dark and terrible prison. "And this is how we rescue the believers", says the Lord; and so we must glorify Him that we may find safety from the flood of sufferings.

One person used to complain bitterly about the croaking of the frogs at night. Angrily he shouted at them: "What's all this racket about? Will you please quiet down! Every night you keep me awake with your 'rak! rak! rak!'" Then the spokesfrog of that pond replied: "Oh son of Adam, I am not lazy like you, sleeping the whole night through, I am keeping this nightly vigil and praising my Lord a hundred thousand times. Are you not ashamed to complain that I keep you from your sleep?"

Yes, we must flee to our Lord in the face of suffering by engaging ourselves in devotion to Him. If you feel yourself being overwhelmed by waves of misery, then say: "Subhanallah, Glory to Allah" and those waves will subside. Glorify your Lord and you will be exalted in the Divine Presence, that is our solution.

The holy Quran observes: *"They forgot their Lord, so He forgot them."*

In reality He never forgets anyone, but as a punishment for our forgetfulness, He permits us to feel forgotten, so that we are overwhelmed by misery. Therefore, every day people are coming to me, trying to unload a heavy burden of misery and the newspapers are bursting with stories of suffering, and nowadays through the television, we are presented with the highlights of the day's disasters and misery. Yes, now we must face it all rather than the small sample we would encounter in our everyday lives, and the disasters we see on television would affect even a heart made of iron.

Nowadays, in order to give people an outlet, to enable them to unburden themselves of some of their pain, a new branch of medicine, psychiatry, has been founded, and those doctors are paid high salaries just for listening to the details of people's mental and emotional chaos. And despite the expense involved in consulting such doctors, their offices are now found on every corner, as green grocers used to be: that is a sign that mental illness is on the increase. The hearts of those psychiatrists must be so expansive to be able to listen to such tales of woe and to try and help their patients, but mostly they too find themselves overwhelmed, and come to me to unload their heavy burdens. My heart sometimes feels as if it too will sink, as I become affected by the misery of people. Sometimes, I may help put someone on the right track by pointing out the causes of his misery, and I am seeking my Lord's support and His forgiveness.

Living Simply, Naturally and Avoiding Waste

Mankind is one extended family. We are all related, and, therefore we share many characteristics, among them a great spiritual power hidden within our being. But our five senses carry us away from ourselves and ensure that we are constantly engaged in our surroundings. As long as we are the slaves of our senses they will draw us into the perpetual pursuit of insatiable sensual desires, and as long as we follow their dictates we cannot gain control of that spiritual power within us.

Because of this tendency, it is essential that anyone seeking to return to himself take his first step on the way of truth by decreasing his desires, by seeking to live an uncomplicated life. We are by nature vain and like to indulge in a lot of self adornment. If people had the financial means, they would wear a new suit of clothes every few hours. In the old days, most people owned perhaps twenty suits of clothes through the course of their lives. Nowadays, it would be impossible for one to be satisfied even with twenty garments at any particular time in his life.

The modern economic system of the West is based on quick production and quick consumption, and that is the epitome of foolishness. Because of the universal predominance of such a system, people in industrialized countries tire quickly and die of weariness – and lifestyle related diseases. The race to produce and consume consumes people, it is a heavy burden on their shoulders.

Therefore, whoever seeks a happy life and spiritual improvement must do as sailors do when a ship is overloaded and in danger of going down in a storm – they throw off the ballast. If you like you may heed my warnings: be wise and move step by step towards simplicity. Don't pursue fashion.

If possible one should eat natural foods, as junk food makes people behave like drunks. We are living in a time in which we are destroying ourselves with our own hands. We have created an economic system geared toward the principle of "quick production, quick consumption", and that is a grave mistake. Since the development of this type of economic system, it has become impossible to fulfill people's needs naturally, to grow food quickly enough without the aid of artificial fertilizers and insecticides, but by means of these violent methods we are destroying the balance of nature.

The teachings of Islam stress the need to avoid waste. If people were to follow only this teaching the ecological balance would be re established. Everywhere in the world people waste food, and in America people throw away a week's worth of food every day. How shall food production keep pace with such waste? By utilizing artificial methods, and these methods in turn breed every kind of illness, economic problems, and psychological problems: all of this is the price of wasting divine favors.

Yesterday I attended a luncheon at which several Islamic scholars were present. They left so much food on their plates! They should not have accepted such large portions if they were not able to eat them, but they did, leaving the surplus to be thrown away. And these are scholars who are well familiar with Islam's teachings about waste, so what should we expect from the common people?

Nowadays, most people's hearts incline towards a wasteful, artificial lifestyle, and away from a life close to nature; therefore, the world's problems are on the increase. I advise any who will pay heed to be friends of nature and not to flee from the countryside to the city. Cities are the plague of the modern world, adversely affecting every aspect of human life – and the bigger the city, the more uninhabitable. Meanwhile, the countryside stands abandoned, as its inhabitants have been hypnotized by the dazzle of city lights.

Our physical bodies are part of nature, and a wise person will seek comfort in closeness to nature, not estrangement from it. Everything in the countryside is purer, and there are fewer illnesses and a generally healthier life. Therefore, I advocate the distribution of the population which is presently clustered in the great cities, throughout the countryside in small communities based on agriculture and decentralized manufacturing. People may work half the day in the fields and half the day in workshops or factories, and their lives would be excellent. If people would live in such a manner they would be healthier and happier.

These huge housing projects which resemble ocean liners are a horror. The government could use the same resources to build a village in the countryside, so that the inhabitants could maintain their human dignity and experience freedom in their surroundings. If it were up to me I would destroy these housing projects, as they are places in which all humanity is taken from humans: jungles, horrible places, centers of criminality. The devil's plan for mankind is to have us jailed in such monstrous buildings, whereas Allah encourages us to use our faculties of reasoning, when He asks: "Is not My earth wide enough that you may migrate thereupon?"

Steady Growth is a Sign of Vitality

How many years have we been coming to London regularly to be with you? For the last thirteen or fourteen years we have been coming here. Tell me, have we called you to anything but the Truth? If we were calling people to ourselves or to some sensations for their egos, many people might come – even more perhaps than now come – but they would not be consistent or perseverant: there would be a high turnover. But no, the same people who joined us then, twelve or fourteen years ago are still with us, and more are coming all the time. They too are staying with us. The ability of a shaykh to help his followers attain stability and a permanent way is a sign of a true follower of the holy Prophet.

There is an episode in the life of the Prophet that illustrates this point. It is important that we study history, as it sharpens our minds and opens the door to insight and wisdom. Therefore, I am advising our friends to study history, even more than religious sciences, to read the history of nations, the history of prophethood and religion, the history of the Prophet's life and early Islamic history, to know also what was happening in the world at the time of the advent of Islam.

Now I will relate to you an episode from early Islamic history that should be useful for us.

The Prophet Muhammad had sent a letter to Heraclius, the Byzantine Emperor, inviting him to Islam. Once, when visiting Damascus (a part of his realm), the emperor instructed his men to bring him any Meccans who might come to Damascus by caravan during his stay, in order to question them about Muhammad, as he was interested in knowing more about him and what people had to say about him.

In due course, the regular summer caravan from Mecca arrived, and its leaders were brought to the presence of his Royal Highness, the emperor. Heraclius was sitting majestically on his throne with a grave expression on his face. To one side were arrayed his generals and to the other bishops and patriarchs. He addressed the Meccans through a translator, saying: "I have received a letter from a man in Mecca who claims that he is a prophet. Who of you is his closest blood relative?" Abu Sufyan stepped forward, saying, "I am his relative." At this time Abu Sufyan was not yet Muslim, and what's more he was the leader of those who were fighting against the Prophet and had forced him to emigrate from his native city to Medina. In other words, he was the leader of those at war with the holy Prophet.

Then the emperor said: "I am going to ask you some questions about that person, and I expect you to provide me with honest, correct answers, as I want to gain a true picture of this man and what he is all about." The emperor addressed the other leaders of the caravan: "And as for you, I would ask you to speak out if your companion gives an incorrect answer and to correct him, for God is Perfect and Correct, and is pleased by those who set things straight."

Later in his life, when Abu Sufyan had become a Muslim, he declared: "I was trembling in front of the emperor, but still I would have told him so many lies to make Muhammad look bad. But he had exhorted my companions to correct me, that one of them might speak up if I lied, and to be exposed as a liar in front of the emperor would have been too shameful for me. Therefore, I was very careful to answer all of his questions correctly."

Heraclius asked Abu Sufyan many questions that are recorded in history books: "Is his following growing steadily? When people come to him do they stay with him or do many go away disenchanted (even though they may be replaced by others)?" Abu Sufyan answered: "Everyone who comes to him stays with him and holds to him more firmly day by day. Their numbers are constantly increasing as the old ones stay and new ones join him."

The emperor exclaimed: "He must be a true prophet, for these are the signs of truth. When seekers of Truth find it, they never leave it. Verily he has been sent with Truth, and his order will grow to perfection. Without a doubt his nation will come and conquer the very ground on which I stand. I wish that I were worthy to serve at his feet."

Then Abu Sufyan said: "Those words of the emperor had an effect on my heart, and from that time my innermost feelings toward the Prophet began to change." We must consider this point: if the holy Prophet had not brought a true message, could his order have grown as it did until it extended from the Far East to the Far West? Can a rotten seed grow? In the time of the Prophet other people arose claiming to be prophets, but can we now see any remnant of their following? But the tree of Islam is always spreading new branches out over the world – that is a sign of its vitality.

Golden Coin and Golden Rule:
Both Have Turned Into Paper

When Allah Almighty created Adam, He caused a rain of trouble to sprinkle on him for forty years, then He caused a rain of ecstasy to shower upon him for one year. Therefore, man may find such a proportion of suffering to pleasure throughout his life. How does our Lord cause trouble to manifest through the course of our lives? Through our contact with other people. We are destined to constantly have to deal with others, most of whom are mainly interested in fulfilling their own desires without much regard for anyone else's well being.

It is our fate to be given a nature that requires social contact with our fellow humans. And even if each person were to have a mountain to himself, in order to remain far removed from the bother and trouble caused by social life, we would find people abandoning their retreats and seeking each other's company in the valleys.

Why is it that people, though drawn to each other, often would like to flee from human association? Each person has his own will and his idea of how things should be done, and it is most difficult to obtain another's compliance with those wishes, to influence him into doing what you want done. If you can come to exercise authority over a small circle of people, the nuclear family for example, your influence decreases immediately when we pass to the next circle of relations, the extended family. And so on down the line: the farther people are removed from your direct influence, the more difficult to assert one's authority or advocate one's position –

and one weak link in the chain will cause the complete rupture of that chain of influence. Therefore, your ability to make others conform to your wishes is limited, and this is a cause of great frustration for people.

When Adam and Eve were alone they were able to agree that Adam would have ultimate authority in matters, and when they had children they deferred to his authority, but when the world started to be populated by his grandchildren and great grandchildren, his authority waned and they became rebellious. By the time he died he had realized how powerless he was.

Everything that happens to mankind in general, every current that passes through us affects our personalities. Some of these currents build in us inner force and rectitude, others cause these qualities to vanish. It is our challenge to face them all and to strengthen our personalities in any case: you must be firm enough to face every event, the good and the bad alike. You may seek to escape from disliked circumstances, but usually, in the process of fleeing you will come up against something even more formidable. We have a saying: "He fled from the rain to the hail." You may affirm the truth of this saying from your own experience. But what can we do? We can only learn forbearance: to increase in spiritual fortitude through being patient with the harm inflicted by others. If we react to every evil we will be burned up with rage, and will have gained nothing. What we need to be able to attack evil is, first of all, a "cool head" not clouded by impulsive rage. This is what all prophets through all epochs have taught.

The great source of suffering in the twentieth century is impatience. Especially in the West patience has become a virtually extinct characteristic, and, contrary to being encouraged by society, even in theory, it is scorned and seen as being the attribute of stupid and exploited people. People in the "free world" are taught that they must demand, and have the right to demand, everything immediately, and ideally, for it to appear in front of them before they ever thought of desiring it – that is efficiency. To call such a society "twentieth century civilization" is a misnomer, for civilized people are patient, and real civilization tries to instill patience by esteeming it as a virtue.

Because this quality is lacking, the higher people's standard of living climbs, the more they come to expect everything to be instantly available to them at the touch of a button or flick of a switch, and when anything God forbid should go wrong, they are infuriated by the delay of what they expect to be instantly provided. It is terrible to even think about the condition people would be in if their systems were to fail on a larger scale: they haven't the slightest idea of how to provide themselves with what they need for their lives. If their machines cease to function they will die – that is all.

An even uglier aspect of this trend is that people are not satisfied just to have everything available at their fingertips, but want to have everything for themselves to the exclusion of others, to have a monopoly of all wealth and pleasure. With such characteristics how shall anyone be happy? Modern education and the values passed through the media give the signal: "Go out and get what you want; if you can grab it, it is yours, that is only fair." What we need to understand is that each has his portion, that what is your is yours and what is his is his. How many of your possessions can you carry on your back? Even a money belt is bothersome: so how shall you carry someone else's portion? If you attempt to eat even one other person's portion you will be sick, and if you wear another's clothing in addition to your own you will be too hot. To begrudge people their portions is excessively stupid, the way to destroy your health and your soul.

We are in need of a different kind of education, an education that teaches us that everything in this life has been apportioned to its owner through divine wisdom, but instead we are encouraging such bad attributes that every good others enjoy is a thorn in our sides.

Once, in the time of Moses, peace be upon him, as he was headed toward Mount Sinai to engage in private discourse with the Lord Almighty, a poor man approached Moses and said: "Oh

Moses, I am so poor. Please ask your Lord to give me something to alleviate my poverty." Moses promised him that he would remember him to his Lord, then went on his way. When Moses addressed his Lord, he pleaded the case of that man as promised, and in response Allah said: "Oh Moses, tell him that whatever he asks I will grant him under the condition that whatever he asks he must also ask for his neighbor, and I will grant it to both of them. Whatever his heart desires – herds, riches, land – I will give them both to him and his neighbor, for I am the Owner of Endless Bounties, I am the Lord, your God."

When Moses descended from Mount Sinai that man was anxiously waiting to hear the Lord's response to his plea. "What news, Moses?" "Good news! The Lord will give you everything you desire, the only condition being that you must ask it for your neighbor as well." Then the man became very angry and said: "If He is not going to give it to me to the exclusion of my neighbor, I am not asking for it, nor will I accept it!"

Now we claim to be civilized people, but who among us may be heard asking: "Oh my Lord, make her as beautiful as I am! I am not happy being a beauty queen while such a nice girl remains ugly." Or who can be heard saying: "Oh my Lord, please give that person a Rolls Royce too! I am ashamed to drive mine unless he has one as well." Or what Prime Minister can be heard saying: "Oh God, make everyone Prime Minister!" I don't think that I can find anyone praying or wishing for these favors on others.

Our egos give us this wild selfishness, but the goal of the Sufi Path is to transform such wild characteristics into beneficial ones, as one may graft bark from a sweet fruit bearing tree onto the trunk of a wild tree that gives only sour fruits. Then, when the graft takes hold, the branches of that wild tree give sweet fruit, although the roots are still wild. Generally, mankind grows as it was planned with no care being taken to transform its sour fruits, and if given no attention, people die in the same condition. You must understand that all of the holy prophets were "gardeners" grafting divine characteristics onto people's wild personalities.

Most of you attending this meeting are Christians and Jews. Christ's mission was to impart divine attributes unto people, and the same is true of all of the prophets of the Old Testament, but you have lost sight of that fact. After Jesus Christ, the Prophet Muhammad came with the same mission, but we lost sight of that too. What was the result of all this heedlessness? Throughout history each group wanted to think of itself as "possessing God to the exclusion of others", and has never liked the idea that God hears the prayers of the other group as well, and considers its merits by His criteria. Not only do our greedy characteristics blind us to the truth of our Lord being the Lord of All, but even within religions so may sects have sprung up, mainly so that people can claim to have the sole possession of God. The result of this has been that Muslims hate Christians and vice versa; but our prophets were not sent to teach us to hate each other: And now Christians hate Christians, and Muslims hate Muslims, and in general every one has turned even on his own brother.

Look, our Lord said: "Tell that person to ask for his neighbor what he asks for himself", that is the commandment which is called the golden rule, but now, just as gold currency has been replaced first by silver and then by paper, so the golden rule has long been out of circulation in our relations. But you must know that your worth is determined by the magnanimity of your heart. In earlier times virtues were recognized as such – though perhaps seldom attained – nowadays they are held in no esteem. People are valued solely according to their beauty or wealth, and one has come to evaluate relationships on the basis of the potential for material gain. This is a shame, and I am asking our Lord to forgive us.

The Difference Between Butchers and Surgeons

A Sufi shaykh must have attained purification of his ego's characteristics to become a shaykh. So, if he is subject to fits of anger he is not a real shaykh, and his teachings will not affect people's hearts. Sometimes however, shaykhs do get angry, but their anger is a barrage directed against people's bad characteristics, not against them personally, and its intention is to help that person rid himself of a bad characteristic that is hindering his spiritual progress. Every bad characteristic presents itself to the shaykh as a target – like the apple on the boy's head in the famous story of William Tell – and an authorized shaykh will target the bad characteristic without harming the man himself.

Another difference between the anger of a shaykh and common anger is that a shaykh will never hold a grudge: he shoots his arrow at the target the moment a bad characteristic appears, and then it is over. Holding grudges is very, very dangerous for all people, for if it continues it becomes a dangerous illness that strikes to the very root of our faith and destroys it. Every time a person displays an objectionable characteristic you may shoot it down, but never assume that you will encounter that characteristic every time you meet that person. Don't say, "There is that person who did such and such yesterday," because today that characteristic has not appeared, and perhaps he has rid himself of it, and you are wronging him in assuming otherwise.

Our grandshaykh was following the holy Prophet in that he never held grudges. If a bad characteristic would appear in a murid he would shoot at it immediately and directly, but with other people he used indirect methods of correcting faults; for it is very dangerous to criticize a person directly, as he may then hold a grudge against you, and we must not invite such a situation upon ourselves or other people. Only saints and small children up to the age of eleven may be able to accept criticism without holding a grudge. After children reach the age of twelve they lose this good quality. You may see small children fight, but when it passes it is over. Some few people never lose this good quality, but in our days it is almost inevitably lost.

When a saintly person meets someone he assumes the best and expects to encounter only good will, but most people are suspicious and anticipate evil when they meet a stranger. Our grandshaykh never anticipated evil from anyone, but when he encountered it, he had divine permission to shoot. Most shaykhs don't even use this method of direct criticism on their murids because of possible harmful reactions. Shaykh Sharafuddin once told our grandshaykh: "If you don't apply poison to external wounds (i.e. medicine for external use only, that would be poison if taken internally) our internally applied medicine might never work."

In the presence of truth the ego raises its head in rebellion, and we must put it down; that is a very delicate task, like surgery. A butcher may cut meat, but he can't perform surgery. The butcher has a knife and so does the surgeon, but what a difference between the two instruments! One of them is used for slaughtering and the other to prolong life. And, as is well known, no one becomes a qualified surgeon simply by reading medical books, but only by being an intern at the side of a master surgeon.

In our time, Muslims are approaching the illnesses they encounter in the West with a butcher's knife, and ignoring Allah's command to call people to truth with wisdom. The Arabs in particular are to blame for the present situation, and most of the scholars from Arab countries are opposing our efforts. Why? Because they are coming with their butcher's knives intending to stab Westerners in the heart, and make sure that all the survivors run for their lives – and I am trying to prevent this. This enrages them, and though they can't accuse me of transgressing the religious law, about Sufis they maintain in general that, "They are calling people to Islam, but have introduced so many innovations." Their criticisms stem from envy, that Sufi "surgeons" are so often successful in helping people over from their illnesses.

In a famous Hadith Qudsi, or holy Tradition, Allah Almighty states that He Himself becomes the eyes, ears and hands of His saints. So how should a Sufi shaykh be oblivious to the needs of the people he encounters? Those Muslim preachers who come to the West without divinely inspired hearing, vision and touch are surely blind, deaf and insensitive (but unfortunately, not dumb).

Once upon a time there was a deaf person. Someone informed his wife that his neighbor was ill. She then communicated this to him through sign language, and he resolved to go and visit the neighbor, but knowing that he could not carry on a normal dialogue, he made the following plan for his visit. I may say 'How are you?' and he will reply, 'I'm feeling a little better.' Then I will say 'May Allah increase it (i.e. your recovery)', and he will say 'thank you.' Then I will sit a while, then ask him, 'Which doctor is attending to you?' and he will say the name of some respected physician and I will reply, 'He is a very good doctor, very suitable for your case.' Then I will sit a while more and ask, 'What medicine have you been taking?', and he will say the name of some drug and I will reply, 'It is very beneficial, keep taking it', then I will offer my salams and go."

So, thus having a fixed scenario in his mind, off he went to the house of his neighbor, knocked on the door and was admitted to the sick man's room. "How are you, oh my neighbor?" he asked. "I'm miserable", replied the sick man. "May Allah increase it", said the deaf man. This vexed the sick man, as you may well imagine. "Who is looking after you?" asked the deaf man. "Azrail, the angel of death", replied the annoyed ill man. "An excellent physician, if he visits you, you should have nothing to worry about", said the deaf man. By now the sick man was furious. "What have you been taking as medicine?" said the deaf man. "Poison", retorted the enraged ill man. "That should be a very useful treatment for you. Now I must go, it has been nice visiting you." The ill man answered, "Go to hell." "Thank you very much, good bye," replied the deaf man.

People who occupy themselves with advising others in matters concerning their eternal lives should be people with open hearts, so that through the eyes of their hearts they may perceive what is relevant and acceptable to the person they are advising. It is not useful just to ignore the fact that the understanding and mentality of people from a different cultural background is drastically different from your own. To be a spiritual advisor is not a question of obtaining degrees in that field, as one would obtain a diploma in chemistry or law; it is a question of subtle changes in the way one perceives people and events, so as to penetrate the defenses and arrive at the reality of a person's inner state. This profession requires a sharp diagnostic eye. You may be a pharmacist in charge of a whole depot of drugs, but you haven't the right to prescribe for ill people. Even if you know the drug required you may not know the dosage, and kill the patient with an overdose.

If we present the medicine to the patient in a form that makes it easier to swallow or taste better, should we be blamed? Is eating iron fillings the only way to get iron into one's system? The holy Prophet said: "I have been sent to approach people tactfully." The meaning of the hadith is that there is no wisdom in meeting people's prejudices head on. Don't seek confrontation, but be wise like the ship's pilot who, when faced with a headwind does not set bow to it and let it push him back, but wisely takes an indirect diagonal course that may be three times as long as the direct one, but can be pursued even in the face of such an unfavorable breeze, a course which will set him towards his goal. The holy Prophet never used the word "No", but we are so busy pointing the finger and saying: "This is forbidden, that won't do." That is not our way, neither was it the way of the Prophet, nor of the great Sufi Masters of history. Some Islamic scholars blame Sufis and call us "innovators", claiming that our methods have no basis in the example set by the holy Prophet. When a seed is newly planted and the first leaves spring forth, these leaves may look somewhat different than the ones that grow later. But we must not cut the later sprouting leaves, saying: "These leaves must be from a different seed." Show me a plant that remains the same throughout its life, and I will show you a plastic plant. Islam was still a sapling in the Prophet's time, and through history has matured into a huge tree whose branches reach from East to West. And even if there are thousands of branches spreading over all peoples and times, they are connected to the root and the main trunk.

Then after some years, a tree develops flowers and fruits as well as leaves. At that point shall we look askance at the whole of mankind as it imbibes the fragrance of the flowers of our tree and as men nourish themselves from the sweet fruits of our tree? Shall we reject fruits and flowers, clinging to a "leaves only" mentality, advocating the destruction of flowers and fruits as innovations? True Islam is not like a hedge that requires a gardener's clippers to keep it square, but like a miraculously expansive and fruit bearing tree – a shelter for all and a source of every delicious fruit.

Aziz Mahmud Hudayi's Reply

An interpreter of dreams must be authorized by his shaykh. Our grandshaykh had permission to interpret dreams and he passed that permission on to us as well. Sultan Ahmed (the Ottoman Sultan who built the famous Blue Mosque in Istanbul) once had a very disturbing dream. Everyone he asked about it expressed his sorrow, for he had dreamt that he was wrestling with the Austrian emperor, and that the emperor pinned him to the ground. But, as he knew that dreams do not always mean what they seem to, he sought someone who could see in it a meaning other than the obvious one.

Then the Prime Minister said to the Sultan, "We must consult my grandshaykh." They wrote down the dream and had a messenger bring it to the shaykh, Aziz Mahmud Hudayi, who is now buried in Uskudar (I always give association in his mosque when I am in Istanbul – it is a blessed place). The messenger arrived at the Tekkia of the shaykh and gave him the envelope. At the same time that the shaykh received the envelope he took another one from his pocket and gave it to the sergeant, saying, "Bring this to the Sultan."

When the messenger returned and was asked what had transpired, the Sultan was amazed to hear that the shaykh had already prepared a reply for him, even before reading the letter. Quickly opening the shaykh's letter, they read: "Oh Sultan, don't worry, for nothing is stronger than the earth, and since your back is earthwards you needn't worry – you are well supported. But as for the emperor, his back is in the air – he is without support. You shall be victorious. (*Sultan Ahmed The First defeated the Austrian Kaiser in the battle of Estergon in 1605.*)

Appreciating Islamic Civilization

Egypt was won to Islam in the time of the Khalifa Umar. Even though Egypt had already been predominantly Christian for a few centuries, a number of pagan customs were still in practice. One of the most abominable of these customs was the belief, preserved from Pharaonic times, that the Nile demanded a bride every year, and, were it deprived of a bride it would refuse to flood, thereby causing a drought. So every year the Egyptians chose the most beautiful virgin in the land, dressed her up in a bridal gown and threw her into the river to drown. At the time of the Islamization of Egypt, the people still believed and practiced this custom.

When the companions of the Prophet heard about this custom they informed the governor that the people were busy choosing and preparing that year's victim. The governor wrote to the Khalifa Umar in order to receive instructions as to how this should be dealt with: whether to let the people go through with their sacrifice or not.

Umar wrote a letter to the Nile via the governor, asking him to throw it into the river. It read: "Oh Nile, if you are running by your own order we are not in need of you, but if you are running by the order of Allah pass on."

The governor delivered the letter to the Nile, and when the Nile flooded as usual, despite the lack of a bride, the people understood that the Nile was but a means for the Lord to bless them and had no will of its own. It was a miracle of Islam to end that bad custom which had cost so many thousands of girls their lives.

In Arabia itself, at the time of the Prophet people used to bury their own infant daughters alive, for no reason other than that they were female. It could be said of them that they were the lowest of mankind; and it is enough proof of the truth of Islam that it transformed a society based on such wickedness, injustice and ignorance into a great civilization guided by the highest spiritual principles within a quarter of a century.

An objective study of history will show that Islam, as brought to the world by the holy Prophet, gave civilization a tremendous push forward. The penetration of Islam from the Arabian Peninsula to the Old World resulted in the establishment of magnificent civilizations based in Damascus, then Baghdad, Spain, Anatolia, Central Asia, Egypt and India. If you look even at the ruins left behind by these civilizations, you will be open mouthed in amazement at the magnificence and harmony of the architecture, and an intimate study of all the aspects of Islamic culture and history, especially Sufism, will breed, must breed admiration.

Whether brought about through victory in military conflicts, through the work of Sufi preachers, or the good example set by Muslim merchants and travelers, the spread of Islam cannot be said to have been an "invasion" in the way that we might refer to the German invasion of France or the French invasion of Germany. No, invasions leave only destruction in their wake: burnt fields, pillaged houses, dead bodies. Islam did not spread as a scourge, but brought with it a magnificent civilization wherever it spread. Can anyone claim that those countries would have developed more quickly without Islam at that juncture in history? Hellenistic thought had reached a dead end, Christian doctrines were in a state of conflict and turmoil, and both had become barren. The advent of Islam brought new life to mankind and a vigorous new direction.

So many misconceptions about Islam have flourished in our time. There are two basic reasons for this. One is that the Muslims of our time are such bad examples of their religion – they are as remote from the truth of Islam as the earth is from the distant stars. The second is that Western people don't bother to take a look at the origins and development of the religion that is so much in the news these days. No one tries to refer to authentic historical sources but blindly accepts the opinions that sensationalist egotistical people in the news media present to them, opinions based on shallow, biased observations of current events charged with hysterical emotion. This situation is much to the detriment of educated Western people who maintain great pretences of objectivity.

The following story should illustrate clearly the likeness of people who rely on television journalism to form their opinions about Islam, rather than seeking accurate historical information. Once upon a time an erudite scholar was traveling through the countryside. He reached a village and went to the mosque to pray. As the prayer began he realized that the village Imam was an ignoramus, making mistakes in the recitation as well as in the movements of the prayer.

The scholar addressed the villagers: "Oh people, you must replace that person with a qualified Imam, for this one doesn't know what he is doing." The villagers were surprised and asked their Imam: "That person tells us that you are ignorant. What do you say?" "He may say what he pleases, but you may put us to the test and see which one is more learned."

Then the villagers gathered like a peasant jury, to let each press their claims and to pass a verdict. If they saw the letter "1" they would have taken it to be a wooden beam. Then the Imam said to the scholar: "Write the word 'ox'." So the scholar put on his glasses and wrote the word 'ox' in very beautiful calligraphy. Meanwhile, the Imam sat down and drew a picture of an ox. Then he asked the peasants: "Tell me, which one is a better ox?" "Yours is", they said, and ran the scholar out of town saying, "You are an imposter! Our Imam is alright and we accept his authority."

Rise at Night for Intimacy with Your Lord

Everyone should strive to become a friend of God, for the Lord never rebuffs the seeker of His intimacy. The main reason for attending a center such as this is to prepare yourself to attain that intimacy. No one can become a friend of God without also becoming a friend of His servants. The attainment of that familiarity and sympathy with the souls of His servants is proof of one's approach to sainthood, for it is easy to claim that one is a friend of God, but not so easy to be in harmony with people.

Perhaps now, during your time here at this center, you may feel closeness with your fellow seekers of truth, but when you return to your countries you will certainly find this harder to realize. When you truly attain the station of friend of God, everyone will be your friend. To succeed in attaining this closeness with people is a sign of one's admittance to the Divine Presence. I don't mean that you become physically attractive or attracted to them – this is not a physical attraction we are talking about – but an attraction through the hearts.

Our grandshaykh once told me a tale about a flower of India that grows only in the most inaccessible places and is, furthermore, always surrounded by snakes. That flower has such an overpoweringly beautiful fragrance that whoever wears it will be loved by one and all. I said to my grandshaykh: "Oh my Master, let me go in search of that flower." He replied, "Oh Nazim Effendi, there is no need for you to go there, for as long as you are vigilant with your Lord after midnight – even for a short time – Allah Almighty will adorn you with an attraction seventy times more powerful than the attraction of that perfume. Even if you just arise during the last watch of the night when everyone is asleep, and even if you don't pray, this miracle will occur and you will become as attractive as that perfume."

Whoever arises at that hour will certainly gain the good graces of his Lord, for that is the time when the Lord looks for the repentance of His servants. Therefore, I advise you all to awaken sometime during the last third of the night: even for five minutes. You must, however, be in a state of ritual purity. Then you must address your Lord: "Oh my Lord, come to me, as I can't come to You." That prayer is enough to give you full protection for that day and makes you a friend of God.

People pass their days coming and going, but in the evening everyone returns to his or her darling. The Lord asks you to be with Him Alone, even for just five minutes in an intimate time of the late night. Who turns to his Lord in the night will find Him near, and will be able to rely upon Him even in the midst of great and terrible events.

Aspiring to Honey Stations

How does a seeker of the Divine Presence attain it? Does one benefit from one's efforts? Is it possible for someone to reach heavenly stations without carrying a heavy burden of worship and spiritual exercises? One of the well known attributes of God is power, His ability to bring about anything He desires, with or without apparent intermediary causes or means. Wings are the means through which flight is made possible, but Allah Almighty is certainly capable of carrying a person from earth to the heavens without any apparent means, without wings. Who can claim that He can't do this?

Nonetheless, Allah has established natural laws, and according to these laws, wings make flight possible. That is the rule, but there are also exceptions. The exceptions, however, are not the concern of people in general, the rule is. Therefore, it is only the smallest handful of people who will reach the level of sainthood instantly without any practice, while it is also undeniably true that some people will sincerely dedicate themselves to pious practices for years, but never get even a foot off the ground.

The Lord Almighty has asked His servants to conduct their behavior according to certain rules, and He says: "Oh My servants, these are instructions, so hold fast to them. It is I who know your destination, so surrender to My will and trust in Me – and trust Me also not to lose or disregard the works you have done for My sake. Don't lose hope, even when you perceive that your deeds are hopelessly deficient, for I can help you when you fall short of your goal. Know that the more difficulties you face in fulfilling the conditions of My servitude, the greater will be your reward."

You have come to this training center seeking spiritual improvement. Not one of you has come for the enjoyment of his physical body. You have come in order to submit yourself to training that you believe will help you develop those wings. You must make an intention to stay a certain length of time – between three and forty days: and you must try to hold to that intention. Don't draw the bucket up the long shaft of the well and drop it just as you are about to hold it in your hands, saying, "I am fed up."

And what sort of training have you embarked upon? You must ask yourselves this question. A suitable method is like a walking stick: my stick will never be a burden for me as I climb the mountain; rather it is my best helper for that purpose. But should carrying a table up the mountain be the same?

A mountain guide must be able to gauge people's capacities and instruct everyone accordingly so that the practice he prescribes should be like a walking stick. Grand Masters are experts in prescribing practices that are effective in aiding people's progress. Especially in our times, any practice that is not like a lightweight walking stick is sure to be discarded. You may find climbing difficult, but that stick should help you reach the summit, and although it technically adds weight to your body it will never be felt as such. Therefore, in our way, each seeker practices dhikr, prayers and recitations in whatever amount helps him in his climb.

Mountain climbing is not the same sort of exercise as a promenade in the park. You must be aware of that fact, but then you must move. You must never say: "It is such a towering mountain, I can never scale it." When a person says, "I will try", the Lord helps him. But when a person falls into despair, divine support is cut. You must not on the other hand, be so self reliant that you forget just how dependent you are upon divine support.

To simultaneously act and depend on divine support can be compared, for the sake of illustration to pressing the gas pedal of your car. As long as you press the gas pedal you may reasonably expect the car to move forward, but if you don't – well, you should grind to a halt. But you must not feel yourself all powerful there with your foot on the gas pedal, for any number of mishaps can make pressing that gas pedal a useless endeavor. Events beyond your control may send that car tumbling into a deep valley, and the higher you have climbed the more certain you are of being destroyed if you veer off a cliff.

When you have understood this point, that you are always and completely dependent upon divine support, then you may be able to connect to that power for the purpose of moving towards your destination, no matter where you are and in what condition. If there is any point in your coming to this center, it is in your gaining an understanding of this point. If you can make a connection to the ever present current of divine support during your stay here, then you may be able to maintain it when you leave.

Our way is not an easy one, but climbing Mt. Everest earns you more distinction and honor than a promenade in the park. With the support of our Lord all the difficulties encountered on this way should become as nothing. Here it becomes necessary for you to ask yourselves what your intentions are, as all divine power arrives by means of our intentions. As long as you are intending to ask for divine support it will never fail to reach you. With the support of your Lord every difficulty should resolve itself.

Even if obstacles appear to loom ahead as huge mountains, don't worry, but know and believe that your Lord's support will enable you to pulverize them. There is a tradition of our holy Prophet: *"The aspiration of men can even uproot mountains."*

Once there was a prophet who was ordered in a dream to swallow the first thing he encountered on his journey the next morning. Upon awakening he braced himself to try and fulfill this tall order. He stepped out of the door and, lo and behold, a gigantic mountain loomed in front of him. He said to himself: "I am the servant and He is the Lord. It is for Him to order and for me to obey. There is no power to change anything except with Him." And so he made the intention to swallow the whole mountain.

Nothing is unchangeable. The Lord may change anything, but when a person despairs of any change in a difficult or impossible situation, quickly that support leaves him and he can't do anything.

That prophet put his trust in God and went towards the mountain. But instead of the mountain looming larger and larger as he approached, it dwindled, as if it were receding into the distance, and by the time he arrived, it had diminished to the size of a small morsel, which he quickly put in his mouth. He had never tasted anything so sweet in his life. That is the reward of those who persevere in trusting God, a pleasure that defies description.

Yes, you must persevere. Don't be like a person who never tastes honey because he fears the sting of the bee. He who is truly enamored of the taste of honey will be daring, and even if he is stung, he will take the honey and run – he won't drop it and run! Yes, there are honey stations in the Divine Presence.

A Lesson From Ibn Arabi's Fall Off His Donkey

Once Shaykh Muhyuddin ibn al Arabi was riding on a donkey (at that time owning a donkey was like owning a Rolls Royce in our time – not everyone could afford one!) surrounded by his disciples, passing through the countryside in silence. All of a sudden, the donkey bucked, and Shaykh Muhyuddin fell to the ground, but his foot caught in the stirrup so that, for a few paces, the donkey dragged him along on his face. Then the disciples rushed upon the donkey to free their Shaykh from this dangerous and undistinguished position, but he prevented them, saying: "Wait a moment until it becomes clear to me in what verse of the holy Quran this event is mentioned." In great distress the murids waited, obeying his wishes, until after a few moments he said: "Alright, now you may free me." So they set him back on the donkey and continued on their way.

Shaykh Muhyuddin was one of those who received the light of perception with which he could discover meanings hidden in the holy Quran, as Allah Almighty says in the Quran:

"Oh people, you may find everything in this Quran: large and small, wet and dry."

Even this meeting must be mentioned there and also what we are saying. Perhaps to some of us this seems to be quite a claim, but just consider a drop of water: you may look and say: "This is just a drop of water, nothing more." But were you to put that drop under a microscope, you would be presented with quite a different picture. Because your view has changed, so has your thought, and you would say: "That drop is a key, and so many things are swimming in it." Where are they? You can't see them with the naked eye, but with the microscope you can see millions of bacteria, and even that is only a small number compared to what we know to be inside that drop, too small to detect with a simple microscope. Even with a microscope we are unable to see the molecules of water consisting of two atoms of hydrogen and one of oxygen: even with an electronic microscope you can't see this. And these atoms themselves consist of nuclei and electrons.

From ignorance one may say: "What is this talk? That is only a single drop of water", but science confirms what we say. The same is true of the holy Quran, for it was revealed as a guide to all mankind, not just to a few people living at the time of the holy Prophet in Mecca and Medina. It was given to all mankind for all epochs, and if life were to continue eternally on earth, the holy Quran would still be relevant to the lives of those people of the future. Therefore, everyone must be able to derive benefit from the Ocean of the holy Quran but we are so pre occupied with trivia that it is impossible for us to see for ourselves. If however, we can concentrate our spiritual powers we will have no trouble recognizing subtle signs.

The holy Prophet himself had the most complete knowledge of the inner meanings of the holy Quran, because of the divine attributes of perception that the Lord bestowed upon him. After him, the Friends of God, like Shaykh Muhyuddin knew that all that occurs is predestined and does not happen by chance or accident. You can't take one step out of that "divine program" – it is impossible. When you understand this point you may live in contentment, and say: "I move in accordance with my Lord's will, and though I may make an intention to do something with my will, if He does not desire it to reach fruition, His will shall overcome mine." And the same is true for something you would never desire, like falling off of a donkey. If it is written for you nothing can prevent it.

Then Shaykh Muhyuddin recited the holy verse: "Say: Nothing will befall us except what Allah has written for us. He is our Lord."

You must believe that He Almighty is your Protector, your Savior, and that He is guiding all things in the best of ways. He Almighty has informed us that this world is only a place of trials, that it is not all and everything, only a prelude to eternal life, therefore we must not blame Him for the vicissitudes of life, nor hate Him for creating a world that abounds in death, suffering and injustice. Rather, we must believe in His promise of final justice, and do our best to advocate justice in this realm, as He Almighty has ordered us: "Strive toward good actions." We must not believe that our Lord has destined evil for us.

We must surrender to His will, and we will attain inner peace, having the burden of the "worry for the morrow" lifted from our shoulders. Whoever believes that God is his Savior feels himself in the best of hands, and will not succumb to hopelessness. Look, as long as you are a conscientious parent, your daughter is not too concerned about where her next meal is going to come from, nor whether she will have a warm bed to sleep in tonight. And though as a good parent you may be training her to take on responsibility, requiring her to be of use in the kitchen or to make her own bed, everything is in order because you are overseeing her efforts. In the same way our Lord provides us with all we need in our lives and the intelligence to use what He provides, overseeing our actions. We must, therefore, be at least as confident about our daily sustenance as that little girl.

This is the nature of our relationship with our Lord: He wills and we intend to follow His will. If we are mad enough to oppose His will, that is our freedom of choice. Yes, He permits us, if we so desire, to declare in a boastful and obstinate way: "I'm going to do what I want." But we are then only like people who are on a ship, walking from bow to stern, thinking that we are advancing in the opposite direction of the ship's course.

The holy Quran says: "He is the One guiding everything in its proper direction." He who understands this will never indulge in saying, "If only." One of the companions of the Prophet used to say: "I would rather eat fire than say 'if only.'" Whoever can leave that way of thinking behind him has found safety in surrender, and should find a whole new horizon opening out in front of him, a horizon free of envy, doubt, regret and worry.

Question: How can we decide or be responsible for anything in our lives, when it is predestined whether we will go right or left?

Shaykh Nazim: Everything must be pre destined, but, as we are mankind, Allah Almighty's most highly honored creatures, we have been honored, and tested with the granting of our own personal will. We are not like other creatures, behaving strictly according to instinct, but have been honored with the ability to consciously decide what we will do: whether we will try to accord with what we know to be His command (which has been revealed to us through His holy books) or whether we try to rebel and go the destructive path.

As I said, we must always assume that our Lord has decreed the best for us, and we must never, therefore, excuse ourselves, saying: "God willed me to do evil." We have our own personal will, and we must do our best with it, but whatever the case may be, we never escape our destiny, but move through it.

The train comes to a fork in the tracks: one track leads to Germany and the other to Switzerland. The driver gives a signal as to which way he wants to go, and the switchman cooperates by putting him on whichever track he desires. That is an honor for us as human beings, that we are not animals to be tied and carried.

The best attitude is for us to say to our Lord: "Inspire me to do what is best." For example, our brother offered to take me for a ride in these mountains. Since he knows these mountains best I will not tell him where to go, but will trust him to take me the most scenic route with the loveliest panorama. I left my will to his, and he is taking me and I trust that I should be pleased when I follow him. If I were to exercise my will and tell him where to go, I am sure that we would be lost very soon. He may ask me which of two scenic drives I prefer and describe them, but he is not going to drive me over a cliff.

We are heavenly creatures but tied to earth, and to know what our Lord desires of us we must develop wings. To know your Lord's will you must cut yourself off from thoughts of this world, and, if only for one minute, put yourself in the presence of your Lord, and ask Him to show you the right way to follow in any matter. He Almighty may show you a red or a green light, that you may know whether to stop or to proceed.

You must address your Lord: "Oh my Lord, You are powerful enough to do everything, while I am completely powerless. You know everything and I know nothing. I am in doubt about such and such a matter facing me in my life. Oh my Lord, if it is good for me open up the way to it, and if it is harmful please keep it from me. And I am asking You, Oh my Lord, for a clear sign to guide me in this matter."

But to do this you must be serious, and it must be a matter of real importance; then, you must be genuinely confounded and open to guidance. You must take a shower and then go to a silent place where you won't be disturbed, and ask your Lord for guidance. This is a method that anyone who is bewildered about his future course may use, and he should receive a clear signal in a dream or waking. There is only one condition: that you must not ask about anything that is already quite clearly indicated. If you come to a street that says "One Way" with an arrow pointing in the opposite direction, or a sign that says "Dead End", the signs are clear and there is no need to ask. There is no need to clarify what is already clear, but when you are confused ask your Lord and He will honor you with an answer.

The Real Light of Faith

Our grandshaykh once related to me an incident from the First World War, when he was in the Dardanelles fighting for the Ottoman Khalifa. An Armenian sergeant who was employed in the service of the Ottoman Empire, addressed a fellow sergeant, a Muslim, saying: "Are you Muslim?" "Of course I am," he answered. "Is it enough to declare that you are Muslim? I can also say that. Now, is there any difference between you and me?" The Muslim sergeant said, "I believe in the unity of God, in His prophets, His books, His angels, the Judgment Day and the rule of destiny." The Armenian sergeant replied: "I may state my belief in all that you have stated. Now, what is the difference between us?"

Our grandshaykh used to comment about the difficulties between Armenian people and Muslims, saying what a shame it was and what a tragic turn of events, caused by the actions of evil men. Earlier on in the history of the Ottoman Empire, Armenian Christians were living with Muslims side by side, and they knew Islam as we know it, only that they were keeping their faith through Christianity.

Then our grandshaykh came and said to the Armenian sergeant: "Oh my friend, are you sincerely seeking an answer to your question? If so, then I may explain the difference between lip service and reality. When a person states his belief in God, His prophets, His revelations, His angels, the Judgment Day and destiny with real sincerity of heart, nothing will block the penetration of his vision to the heart of all things. If he looks down at earth he will not be prevented from seeing what lies beneath it. If he looks up at the heavens, the distances should not hinder him from seeing the seven heavens. He who sees with the light of faith should, when he turns to the East, see all the way to the Far East, and likewise in any direction. When he turns toward Mecca in his prayers he should see the house of God before his very eyes. Then the Armenian sergeant said: "Yes, that is the faith I am seeking," and he kissed Grandshaykh's hands, and completed his faith by adding sincere intention to his verbal affirmation of faith. If a person is granted real faith – neither distance nor darkness nor huge mountains can block his view – his light penetrates.

Fulfilling Our God Given Potential: The Story of Sunbul Effendi

Sunbul Effendi was a grandshaykh who lived in Constantinople around four hundred years ago. He had many murids: some were old and had been with him for many years, but there was one young murid who had only recently joined the shaykh, and it was apparent to everyone that the shaykh favored this young man over all of them and intended to groom him as his successor.

This situation awakened envy in the hearts of some of the old timers. If not for envy there would be no hell. Envy is a fire, but no one sees its flames but saints: and they see it jump from one heart to another and cover the whole world. Only very few people are safe from these flames, flames that make the world a hell.

Sunbul Effendi could perceive the envy of their hearts, though they were very careful to conceal it, even from themselves, and he knew that it was necessary for him to show them why he was giving special attention to the young murid, and why he was the most suited to be the shaykh's successor. So he asked one of the older murids, "I want to ask you a hypothetical question. Of course it is impossible that such a thing could ever be, but if you were the Lord of this world, and had the reins of divine power in your hands, what would you do, what decrees would you issue?" "Well, of course such a thing is impossible, glorified be God! However, if you ask me to imagine this strictly hypothetically, I would, if I could, put an end to all public manifestations of indecency. I would close every cabaret, every bar, and even every coffee house as coffee houses are the soil in which the seed of evil is planted, to be transplanted at a later time into bars." The shaykh said: "That is very proper, commendable actions no doubt."

Then he asked another old timer what he would do if he were so empowered. He said: "I would make sure that every Muslim woman covers herself properly and behaves modestly. I would not tolerate a single hair showing from beneath their scarves. Everything would be put in order, and I would make my point clear by lining the streets with sword and baton carrying enforcers of the law." "Oh my son," said the shaykh, "you are a very important person."

Then he asked the young murid what he would do were he empowered to rule the world from on high. "Oh my Master, if I were in that position I would have everything continue upon the course that it is presently on. I would never intervene to alter the forces of destiny." Then the shaykh said: "My son, you have supplied the correct answer."

The understanding of that young murid reflected wisdom, for the wise know that it is God's purpose to allow both good and evil to flourish. Otherwise, how would good people prove their goodness? If there were no temptation people would not have to choose to resist it or succumb to it. In such a case human beings would forfeit the one thing that distinguishes them from the rest of God's creatures, and a great honor that has been bestowed upon us.

God has established a balance in this life, a balance between good and evil, faith and unbelief, obedience and rebellion. If the world were suddenly filled with obedient people that balance would be thrown off center. Our Lord has given us free will to choose this way or that, and it is in the exercising of that will that we fulfill our potential. Nothing pleases Allah more than repentance, than exercising our willpower to turn away from the pull of the lower self. Without willpower we are but beasts of the field. So, if not for evil we would not have access to our highest potential. Because the young murid had understood that both good and evil are necessary, and are both the will of God, his vision was more penetrating than that of the others. This made him eligible for the station of deputy, and qualified him to train future murids. He who surrenders to God's will and sees it behind all events has gained perfect vision.

We are not pleased with the actions of evildoers, and we must try as best we can to set wrongs aright. But we must see everything with the eye of wisdom and be as patient as we can in the face of people's bad actions, understanding that the Lord has allowed them to follow their own bad impulses into folly. We must not hate them, but hope that the wrongness of their actions might become apparent to them through the workings of the conscience and mind that Allah has bestowed upon each and every human being. He is "the Turner of Hearts" and it is His wisdom to accomplish this turning of hearts through the granting of freedom to His servants, not by force. But this freedom carries responsibilities, as in the end, it will make us answerable for our actions, and He will ask: Did I not give you a mind and a conscience with which to distinguish between right and wrong? Did I create you as dumb animals? Why did you not use the gifts I gave you, remaining instead unthinking slaves of your egos?

Wisdom dictates the following of the way that leads to perfection. The capacity for following such a way is a divine gift. Not pursuing it means falling short of our potential, and that is a shame and a dishonor for us.

The Final Limit

I ask my Lord to help me to be just and to uphold justice. This is what our Lord asked of mankind from the time of the first man, Adam, up to our time, and it is what will be asked of man until the Last Day. A person who stands for justice is called "Haqqani", and that title is the essential basis of all other honorable ranks in the Divine Presence.

"The day when truth will benefit the truthful."

It means nothing to Allah that you were known in this life as a Muslim, Christian, Jew or Buddhist, but He will be concerned with whether you deserved the title of Haqqani. Those who have been Haqqani in this life are transformed; their very essence adopts divine attributes so that they become "Rabbani" or beings who pertain to the Lord intimately. It is about these people that Allah Almighty says in a holy hadith:

Oh My servant, be obedient to Me and I will make you Rabbani; then you (also) will say to a thing "be" and so will it be.

When one reaches the level of Rabbani, God dresses him in His own attributes and makes him deputy. Then He grants him willpower that is not your own, but His. But the way to attain the station of Rabbani leads through the station of Haqqani, and whoever intends sincerely to be Haqqani will receive guidance from Him.

What is the nature of the station of Rabbani? For those in that station the ocean may be as a puddle, and even the whole world may be a crumb in their hands. Abdul Wahhab ash Shaarani, a great Sufi of Egypt, said that some men of God see the world as a candle and some see it as an atom. A man of God will first be shown the nature of the universe and all of its creatures, then he will learn about the Lord Almighty. Therefore, on his night journey the holy Prophet was shown the whole universe and only thereafter was invited to leave it and enter the realm of absolute truth. He left everything, including his self, and entered the Divine Presence – but only after he had been shown everything about the world did he enter Unity Oceans.

He entered Unity Oceans but he was ordered back to the world to invite all nations to follow him to the Divine Presence. Those who heed his call to ascend to the seven heavens are two separate groups. The first group consists of those who may potentially attain the station of Gabriel. When Gabriel was leading the holy Prophet in his ascension, he stopped at a certain point, for fear of being annihilated in the divine. That station represents the highest attainment possible through the mind. The second group contains those who are prepared to sacrifice everything, even themselves, to attain absolute Unity Oceans. Their station is absolute unity, Ahadiyya, while the station of those who fail to throw off the yoke of mind, form and relativity is the station of Gabriel, the station of awareness of unity, Wahadiyya. The station of Wahadiyya is in Unity Oceans, but it is a "substation." It is, however, the uttermost limit for all but the fewest of seekers.

The way to the station of Ahadiyya, of absolute unity, is one of total inner renunciation of all hopes of being something. Some of our brothers have asked me to open up to them the doors of divine attraction, Jadhbah. It is a kind of a power, but it is not my job to dispense power, but to take it away, that you might be empty handed and thus candidates for the station of Absolute Unity.

If an unprepared person were to receive spiritual power, he would only wreak destruction upon himself and others. A little boy may admire the large horses the police ride, but if we were to mount him on such a horse, do you think that he would be able to control it? Sometimes a father may put his small son on his lap while he drives down a quiet street, and let him steer, but do you think that the father is really letting him drive?

Only those who have subdued their egos may be given any power. A rocket is not launched until all of its systems have been checked many times over – and the flight of each soul to its heavenly destination is much more important than launching a rocket, so don't imagine that grandshaykhs empower their murids easily.

Once, Ubaydullah al Ahrari called one of his murids and said: "Oh Abdullah, go climb that mountain and wait there for me, I am coming after you." The murid climbed the mountain and began to wait. The morning passed, then the afternoon. The sun set and still there was no sign of the shaykh. The next day the dervish waited patiently, but still the shaykh did not come. But his orders were clear, so he waited: a week, a month, a year, five years, seven years. He survived on that mountain as a beast would survive. In the summer he fed himself with berries and in the winter from the bark of trees. When he prayed the birds would alight on his shoulders and at night when he chanted his dhikr the animals would gather around him in a circle.

There he waited for seven years without any news from his grandshaykh. But the grandshaykh had originally received the order to send that murid to the mountain from the holy Prophet, and he was awaiting the order to go up after him. When the order arrived the shaykh went up to the murid's perch in the blink of an eye and said to him. "Oh my son, why have you been waiting here so long? I told you that I was coming, so when I didn't come why didn't you come and see what had happened to me? I could have died or been hurt, I could have been lost on the mountain: so why didn't you search for me?" The murid answered: "Oh my Master, I was ordered to wait for you, not to look for you. You ordered me to wait here until you came and, as the saying goes, 'Whatever a noble person promises, that he will fulfill', so what about you, Oh most noble of mankind! Is it possible for you to promise something and then fail to fulfill it? I would have waited here for you even until the Last Day. A dog will wait for you if you tell him to, so how shall I be less loyal and obedient? Besides, it was not too difficult for me to wait here – at least you came before I died, when you could have left me until that time too. I relied on your word, not on my mind's judgment, as I know that you are caring for me." The murid had understood that his shaykh was not really scolding him for staying there but was testing him by repeating the same arguments and objections that his ego had brought forwards when the shaykh had not appeared when expected.

That murid attained the same level of reliance upon his shaykh and through his shaykh on the Prophet and ultimately on his Lord, that Abraham attained in reliance on his Lord. When Abraham was thrown in the fire by Nimrod, the angel Gabriel came and asked him: "Are you in need of help?" "I am in need of my Lord's help, not yours," replied Abraham. Then Gabriel said: "Then ask your Lord for help." "There is no need for me to ask, for He sees me, looks after me and knows well where I am and of what I am in need."

That murid was on exactly the same level of trust to his shaykh. He knew that his grandshaykh was not a blind person, and therefore, he must be aware of his condition. This is why he answered his shaykh's queries by saying: "Oh my shaykh, I have no doubt that you are keeping me within the scope of your spiritual vision, so why should I apply my mind and will when I have given the reins of my will to you, trusting that you will guide me to my Lord's pleasure. I am in your hands like a dead body in the hands of those who wash it before burial."

Then there appeared a flock of wild doves as an escort for a very large green bird, a bird that appears to murids who have successfully completed their seclusion. That is a sign that the murid is ready to be escorted to the presence of the holy Prophet and the grandshaykhs of his assembly. The holy Prophet ordered Ubaydullah: "Now I have witnessed that your murid is absolutely in control of his ego, you may give him his powers."

The powers received at this point are six:

1. Haqiqat ul Jadhbah (The Secret of Attraction)
2. Haqiqat ul Fayd (The Secret of Emanation, or Outpouring)
3. Haqiqat ut Tawassul (The Secret of Connection)
4. Haqiqat ut Tawajjuh (The Secret of Alignment)
5. Haqiqat ul Irshad (The Secret of Guidance)
6. Haqiqat ut Tayy (The Secret of Folding Space)

Until the holy Prophet appears to the grandshaykh and takes upon himself responsibility for the murid, no powers are given. But at that time the floodgates are thrown open.

In our way we must never claim to know anything or to be anything, because dissolution in Unity Oceans requires the abandonment of all pretentiousness. Most people, on the contrary, spend their life energy on futile attempts to grasp something in their hands. However, when they open their hands to see what they have, they realize that they never caught it, or even if they did, it flies away as soon as they open their hands. Even seekers of truth sometimes attempt a "catch" by trying to reach a spiritual station for the sake of their egos. In this case seekers have not completely renounced self aggrandizement, but in accordance with their level they may attain good in this life and the next, but not that ultimate station of Ahadiyya. Only he who abandons the covetousness of this life and the next will be given pleasure that no one can imagine.

A murid becomes eligible for these powers when he becomes free of his ego's tyranny. When they are granted he is a free man, forever free of the limitations of time and space. Time and space are the illusions which now bind us. When we are free they are at our command.

The Power of Attraction is the power which enabled the saintly advisor of King Solomon to bring the throne of the Queen of Sheba to Jerusalem from Yemen in the time it takes for an eye to blink, or less. (Quran, Chapter 34) This is the power that enables one to draw anything to himself. Inanimate objects are the easiest, people the most difficult.

The Power of Emanation or Outpouring is the power to be the means for the transfer of the experience of the Divine Presence to the murid. It is all embracing light that overflows the brim of the vessel. The holy Prophet is the vessel in which these divine favors are poured and, as they are without end, they flow from his heart to the hearts of saints and from theirs to those of murids.

The Power of Connection is the power to connect at all times to this chain of transmission of divine power and favors. For saints it is the intimate knowledge of the prophet's realities and those of the chain of shaykhs leading to him. For those who are yet aspiring to that station it is the daily invocation of the names of those grandshaykhs leading up to the holy Prophet. In our time, the time when the advent of Imam al Mahdi is anticipated, many more people will have access to this power than ever before.

The Power of Alignment enables the shaykh to turn his heart towards the hearts of his murids at any given time, and to turn their hearts towards their destinations. If he can't do this then it is meaningless to say that he is a shaykh. The first step is in his turning the heart of the murid towards his own; after this it will be possible to turn it onwards.

The Power of Guidance is the power to lead one on his way to his destination once he has been turned toward the direction through the Power of Alignment. For example, if you arrive at Heathrow Airport it is not enough, you must be lead or given directions to arrive at your specific destination in London. Therefore, being turned in the direction is only the first step, the door of the maze; you must be helped on through it.

The Power of "Folding Space" is the power to travel at will anywhere in the universe without actually traveling the distance, but rather by "rolling it up" like a parchment. Such a thing is unattainable except for those who have subdued the physical body absolutely. Presently our souls are encased in our physical bodies. The secret of this power is, by bringing the physical body under control it becomes encased in the spiritual body, and the movement of the spiritual body is not cumbersome like that of this body. What is the speed of a donkey compared to the speed of light? The speed of light is like a donkey compared to the speed of the spiritual body.

The Station of Unity

"Oh my Lord, I ask You to grant me understanding, and to enable me, Oh my Lord, to make others understand." (A prayer of Prophet Muhammad, peace be upon him)

Every time I address people I silently make this supplication, as I know that only he who himself understands can teach people anything useful. A visitor recently told me about a spiritual teacher whose lectures and writings were so difficult that no one understood what he was saying. It is not a sign of a man's understanding that his teachings be incomprehensible; a man of understanding will always try to make himself well understood by using clear and straightforward speech, adjusting to the level of his audience, and he will try to address as broad an audience as possible, otherwise his words will be scattered with the winds.

Even Allah Almighty, the Lord of all creatures, the Master of existence, in all His glory and greatness condescends to the level of His creatures. This is called "Tanazzulat Subhani" or, as close as it can be translated, "the Condescension of Glory" (or "the Condescension of the Glorious One"). You may find Him Almighty with His creatures on every level.

If He were not with an ant and knew not the conditions in which that ant lives and what are its needs, He could not – by definition – be the Lord of that ant. He, the Lord of all, in His knowledge, made mankind the most distinguished of His creatures. Is it, therefore, too much to say that He is with us? "Does the Creator not know what He created?" asks the Lord, that we may understand His Omniscience, and that being the Lord of all creation does not detract from Him being with each individual creature.

The holy prophets and their Inheritors in every age have been endowed with knowledge of divine realities which is hidden from the rest of humanity, and it is their main duty to make these realities comprehensible to mankind in general, and to individual people in whatever way possible, in accordance with the respective levels and capabilities of those people. As the teachers of humanity they have been granted the ability to communicate in this manner: to speak directly to people's hearts. This they have been granted from the attributes of their Lord. But only prophets and their true inheritors may find such flexibility available to them; for others it is very difficult to address anyone other than those who share with them a similar background and manner of perception. But divine teachers may be to every people what they need, may say what they need to hear; that is why people of varying backgrounds and ranks in life may all find peace with the same man and follow him.

A Concorde could never land on the roof of this building, but a helicopter could. Most scholars are like Concordes; so proud of their immense wingspans, streamlined form and speed. Only a few statesmen and tycoons – men and women of distinction and endowed with great wealth – may enter and ride Concordes. So scholars may speak and write for the appreciation of other scholars. Concordes fly at tremendous speeds and require huge runways at international airports to land, but a helicopter can land anywhere, even sometimes at sea, and can always hover in mid air while lowering a lifeline to people trapped by a fire. So divine teachers are accessible to everyone in every situation, whereas Concordes might crash in a place where only helicopters can reach to rescue the survivors. Therefore, I am not leaving them on the tops of the Himalayan Mountains, but bringing them to safety.

Seekers of Truth must look for those qualities in a teacher who purports to be addressing subjects related to the divine. Otherwise they will be pursuing useless studies, and, according to the holy Prophet, a sign of a person's perfection in Islam is his abandonment of useless activities ("that which doesn't concern him").

Our guest mentioned that this scholar was addressing the topic of "fana and baqa", or "annihilation and permanence in the divine." I think that no one except those who have arrived at these stations is qualified to speak of them; otherwise his description will be like that of a person who has never tasted honey trying to describe its taste from what he has read about it to others who have been deprived of honey. Or it will be like asking a little boy about the pleasures of a honeymoon... useless.

These topics are oceans. When you melt, dissolving in the Unity Ocean of Allah Almighty, then you may understand the meaning of "Fana fillah" (Annihilation in Allah). When you abandon your position as a being in existence, when you become as a drop of rain falling from the sky and are immersed, united in that ocean of divine unity, then no one can ask where that drop has gone: the drop became an ocean.

As long as the drop is falling, it continues to say: "I am something", but when it reaches that ocean, it looks and says: "Where am I? I am finished. I am with Him. I am here, but not here; only He is here, but I am now with Him. I am in His Ocean. I feel this, but no more can it be said that I am a drop, this drop has become an ocean." That is only a very simple description of annihilation in God.

"Baqa" or permanence, is to be with Him always. In such a station your personality does not appear; what appears is only divine existence. You have been dressed in divine Unity. That is the "station of Unity", "Maqam at Tawhid". What Baqa means is that you will never lose sight, hearing, feeling, knowing, understanding, but these stations will be without limits. We must try to attain these stations, but the Way is difficult and requires severe training.

One of the aspects of that training is to try and see everything as proceeding from Him Alone. This is the sixth pillar of faith in Islam: the belief that everything that happens in this world, the good and the bad alike, are from God. This is referred to as "Tawhid al Af'al" or "The Unity of Actions." The way to begin to realize this point is to remember the Source of all events, Allah Almighty, when events occur, and not to occupy one's self with blaming or lauding those who are not really the causes of events, only the instruments to their occurrence. This means that if Ahmed comes and gives you a pound coin and then Fulan comes and slaps you and takes it away, you don't think of Ahmed as the giver of the money, nor of Fulan as a thief. If you think like this you have fallen from that high level of faith. You must perceive the hand of Allah behind both hands – that which giveth and that which taketh away – as He is the creator of the actions of people.

When someone is generous or kind to you, you must remember that it was your Lord who sent him with that favor, and you must thank your Lord. But at the same time you are going to say: "Thank you" to that person, as without giving thanks to the carrier of that blessing your thanks to its origin is not going to be complete. Therefore the holy Prophet said: "Who thanks not people thanks not Allah." Our Prophet, upon whom be peace, is advising us strongly that we should not allow our vision of unity to distract us from perfecting our politeness with our fellow men. But you know that it is your Lord who sent him, and you are not forgetting that under any circumstances. And when you see that Ahmed has filled your hands with gold, you must say to him: "Oh thanks to your Lord, who sent you with favors for me, and thank you for faithfully delivering what was entrusted to you."

And when that robber Fulan comes, hits you and takes all the money, don't be angry with him! Yes, the divine law, the Shari'ah, permits you to retrieve that money if you can, and prescribes a punishment to be meted out by the society as well, but if you are on the way of Unity, then you must regard that action as coming to you from Allah Almighty too. He Alone sent that man to rob you, because the Creator of every action is only One: Allah Almighty.

Because it is not possible for all people to aspire to this high level of faith in which God's Hand is seen behind every event, in one verse of the holy Quran Allah Almighty condones "a life for a life" in the case of murder, and goes on to call those who are capable of it to "turn the other cheek." These are the levels, respectively, of Shari'ah, the Law, and Tariqah, the Path. Based on this verse, therefore, the Islamic Law concerning murder is balanced, making concession for the normal human feelings for vengeance in the face of such an abominable crime. Islam allows for execution of the duly convicted murderer, and in this way assuages the feelings of the close relatives, thus preventing extended blood feuds. The law also allows for the payment of blood money in lieu of execution, to be paid to the victim's close relatives. Lastly the verse calls those who are seeking forgiveness, saying: "And whoso forgives and promotes understanding, his reward is incumbent on his Lord."

What Allah is saying to seekers of Absolute Truth is: "Now forgive him, because I sent him to do that action." Then you realize that, in reality, there is no question of guilt nor need for revenge. But that is not the common level. That is the level to be striven for, and it is beyond us to forgive in such a manner because our egos are like volcanoes.

Now people may be very polite in their everyday dealings, as long as everyone behaves in accordance with their expectations and everything falls into place according to plan; but should, God forbid, the smallest thing go wrong – for example a small error in driving, even one that causes no accident – for such a small reason one may hear the ugliest obscenities pour from their mouths like a lava eruption. That ego makes people dangerously ill, and now that people are totally under their egos' command, where can you find the tolerance described in that holy verse of the Quran?

So much hate and frustration is pent up in people – I see it in their looks – and so often a scapegoat is sought upon whom to release that torrent, and the best, the tried and true scapegoat throughout the world is always the "foreigner"; so I am quick to assure people here in the West: "We are just here as your guests. This is your homeland." But is it? You can't stay here either except in your graves. Your homeland is the grave, not above ground. Thank God, no one is begrudging us cemetery plots; no one is trying to prevent our being buried. The gravedigger wipes the dirt off his hands and goes away, and the earth accepts us indiscriminately; but people on the earth are busy making distinctions, and therefore, that high level of acceptance of actions as coming from God is rarely found. But He teaches us the lesson nonetheless, saying: "You must understand who I am; I am the Creator of people and their works, understand this, that you may attain peace and finally leave behind your quarrelsomeness."

Once I was in Mecca with our grandshaykh making Tawaf (circumambulating) the House of Allah, the Kaba. Grandshaykh said to me: "Look up!" When I looked up I saw above the heads of the people another group of worshippers performing their Tawaf; but these people were of a different class: calm, peaceful and graceful. They too were of mankind, not Angels, but they were the ones who had reached the level of seeing every action as issuing from Allah Almighty, therefore they left the level of earthly struggle.

But, meanwhile, back on the ground, amidst the throng, with those who lack such certainty, we were being pushed, shoved and trampled upon. Some groups locked arms and shoved straight through the crowd, full speed ahead, sending all who were unfortunate enough to fall in their path flying through the air, like discarded banana peels. Elbows in my ribs, heels on my toes...but above us, the ones who concur with God's will have no need for earth under their feet. Now, perhaps, you are thinking that such a thing is impossible, that I am telling a "tall tale", but yet, when you are told that airplanes fly you think nothing of it. If man can make metal fly, cannot God make man fly? They are at peace with their Lord and with everything in creation; therefore, everything carries them.

And so, we have been shown a higher way, the vision of Unity, and we have been asked to be patient with those events that are not to our liking, remembering their source. This is the best training for our egos. Undergo this training or you will struggle fruitlessly – up to the grave. We are being trained by our Lord to recognize the Unity of Actions, so that we can come to understand the Unity of His holy names, which leads us to the knowledge of the Unity of His holy attributes. That knowledge will prepare us for that ultimate dive into the Unity Ocean of Allah Almighty's essence. That is the final goal. That raindrop falls, and it will not emerge again ever – and it is content because it has just gained everything eternally, forever.

Therefore, Allah Almighty addresses mankind, saying: "Oh man, verily you are striving towards your Lord, and you will meet Him." He Almighty is teaching us that all our striving on earth, our running from East to West, here and there, night and day, is, unwittingly, nothing else than our race towards our Lord's endless Unity Ocean, but we can't now understand. Our souls long for our Lord; therefore we move, and there is nowhere to move save towards the One.

No One is Refused

Today, as I was praying, an important point appeared in the mirror of my heart, a subject that needs to be addressed. What is the position of every single person toward the rest of humanity and the rest of creation in general? Each person, each being, is by nature self centered, though constantly interacting with others in his surroundings. Everybody divides his fellow beings into distinct categories: those having more in common with himself and others more in opposition – and the less in common the more critical the questions become. So as a follower of a certain religion, you must ask yourself, what your attitude towards members of other religions will be. As a man, what kind of attitude do you have towards women, or as a woman towards men? As an elderly person towards the young, or as a youth towards the elderly? As a wealthy person towards the poor, or as a poor man towards the wealthy? As a literate person towards the illiterate? What is your attitude as a human being towards animals, plants, inanimate objects, everything in existence?

The holy Prophet, Muhammad, upon whom be peace, gave guidance to mankind in this matter when he said: "My Lord has taught me to show respect to all, to maintain a high level of good manners, and my Lord has perfected His teaching." Now we need to know what those best manners are, and how they help us to show respect to all creatures in accordance with their respective levels, for, while Allah Almighty has made all creatures worthy of respect, He has especially honored mankind. We are invited to realize the full potential of that honor by perfecting our relations with all that surrounds us.

This perfection calls for a balance in our relations, along with the perception of the differences between beings and an ability to adjust our behavior according to those distinctions. This is because Allah's creatures, most especially men, are not factory productions, mass produced and cut out of the same mold. Each person has his own unique form, characteristics and capabilities – you can't find two exactly identical people; even identical twins may differ drastically in character. Everyone carries something distinct, and we must observe these varying and distinguishing marks, that thereby we may receive divine wisdom, and marvel at the power of our Lord, for who else could create such diversity? Whether you look around you at your fellow men, or at the stars in the sky, you will know, by their infinite variations that only God could have created the universe.

Human beings, the "Crown of Creation", are candidates for the honorable rank of "Deputy of Allah on earth." We are beings who have been endowed with the potential for uncovering a great secret within ourselves. If in heedlessness we do not strive for it, it will remain deeply hidden within ourselves. What is the great secret within man that he must discover to attain this rank? It is to understand that you are a manifestation of one of our Lord's endless divine attributes. Each person manifests a distinct attribute, no matter how many billions of people appear and disappear from this earth; each one manifests a unique aspect of the divine reality. Each divine attribute is distinct and, when fully unveiled, equally divine. Therefore, our Lord is oblivious to our outward forms but is always mindful of the states of our hearts, as the heart of each man is a throne from among the endless thrones of Allah Almighty. That heart is not the organ in our chests; it is only represented by it as a figure of speech. In your real heart, your "heart of hearts", there is a throne and He Almighty appears on that throne through a distinct attribute that manifests in you, and nowhere else in creation.

Therefore, you must respect everyone in existence, as in reality that respect is the respect for your Lord within him. That is the way our Prophet treated people, the way taught by real Islam; a deviance from this "Way of best manner" is a dangerous innovation (bid'a) of high degree. The respect that we must show towards our fellow human beings is such that, should a baby be born, take three breaths and die, we must name him, wash his body and pray over him the funeral prayers; and if there is no one else to perform those rites, even the Sultan himself is required to do so, even if that baby is born to the lowest class of his subjects.

And what if the living or the dead be of another religion or without religion, do we show them less respect? One day the holy Prophet was sitting with his companions when a funeral procession passed by. The holy Prophet stood up in a sign of respect to that departed soul. One of the companions said: "Oh messenger of God, that is the body of one of the heathens. Are you showing respect to such people?" It was a sign of bad manners for that companion to say this, and he immediately regretted it. Does the Prophet not know whether that dead person and those of the procession are Muslims or idol worshippers? If not, how can he be a prophet? But as the companions were at different levels of understanding and manners, building gradually towards perfection, the Prophet was always patient with those who showed such a challenging attitude; he explained his actions to that companion according to the level of his understanding – which was the common level. And how difficult for the common believer, whose human feelings are caught in the ebb and flow of daily events to understand how the Prophet gave this respect for people who were actively engaged in oppressing the Muslims – killing and boycotting them, and generally showing abominable qualities! How difficult for the common people to make a distinction between people's bad actions and the divine realities hidden and veiled, yet present and untouched, in their heart of hearts, and in this way to understand why you must not hate your enemies! Such understanding makes a person eligible to receive divine secrets, and a category of knowledge the holy Prophet was instructed to reveal only to initiates.

Therefore, to guide that companion in the general direction of this reality while not revealing to him that which he could not comprehend, the holy Prophet told him: "Yes, these are unbelievers, but you must know that each one has Angels accompanying him, recording his good and bad deeds, and the Angel of Death, Azrail, is accompanying the dead man as well; I am standing out of respect for those Angels." In this way the holy Prophet instructed all Muslims to show respect to all people living and dead, no matter how terrible their actions might be.

Mawlana Jalaluddin Rumi, an Islamic saint known throughout East and West (and the author of the epic Sufi poem, the Mathnawi) was once crossing a marketplace when a priest passed by and bowed his head in respect. Mawlana returned this gesture, bowing even lower, from the waist. The people asked him: "How is it that you bowed in front of that priest (who represents a religion that failed to recognize the holy Prophet of Islam)?" In Islam, bowing is a gesture generally reserved for the worship of God, other signs of respect being used more commonly.

Then Mawlana answered them, on a level that accorded with their understanding: "That priest was humbling himself in front of us. He is Christian, we are Muslim; and Islam represents the completion of every goodness found in Christianity. Therefore, if he is humble we must strive to be even more humble."

This explanation is true, but on a deeper level, this reciprocation may be understood as respect to the real personality, the divine personality of that priest – and it is only He Almighty who dresses His servants in differing outward forms and predisposes them for different kinds of actions. Mawlana recognized that it was his Lord who dressed him as a Shaykh and dressed that man as a priest; and if He wills, He can cause them to change roles, for each of their hearts to cling to the other's religion in the blink of an eye; and who can say what Allah will do? What is beneath all these clothes but the throne of Allah, in a unique personality manifestation?

In the holy Quran it is related that, when Allah Almighty created Adam, He ordered all the angels to prostrate in front of him. Do you think Allah Almighty was ordering them to worship other than Himself? All of the Angels were able to perceive that divine manifestation in Adam, and bowed down to their Lord by prostrating in front of Adam. But also in attendance was Satan, who was veiled by envy, and said: "What is he that I should worship him: I worship God alone." But Satan could not see what was inside of Adam: all the holy Names of Allah that were to be manifested by all of his descendents. Were those veils of envy to be lifted, he would have been the first to obey. Envy blinds us to this vision, and unhappily, it prevented many of those who represented earlier revealed religions from recognizing the Prophet Muhammad when he came, the veritable brother of the prophets they venerate.

If we can remember that the presence of this divine secret is in people's hearts, and look past their outward forms and actions, we may learn from everything and everyone and increase in wisdom. Only with this vision can we aspire to a magnanimity that will cause good actions to appear from people, for a ray of their divine essence to shine through and encourage the veils of ego to be lifted. Respect of the divine nature in man leads to familiarity between people, and familiarity opens the way to love, and all love belongs to our Lord.

Our main responsibility in life is this: to clean off the bad characteristics that cover our divine personalities, and once we have accomplished this to help others free themselves of that heavy burden. We must always remember the sacrosanct nature of souls. Look, Sayyidina Umar, who was to become the second Khalifah of Islam, came to the holy Prophet with the intention of killing him, but left that meeting with a heart full of love and goodness. He was the same man, the essence of his being never changed, only his attitude did. So, we must always beware of saying: "So and so is a bad person." You can't say that of his real essence, no.

Although we regard the essences of people, we don't accept their bad actions, but "fire upon" them the same way that a surgeon removes a tumor from a patient and leaves healthy tissue inside of him; he knows to distinguish healthy tissue from cancerous tissue and removes only what is dangerous.

That is the method practiced by all the prophets of all revealed religions from the beginning to the end. To help people purify themselves of destructive characteristics was the mission of Moses, of Jesus and also of the seal of prophets Muhammad, who was ordered by his Lord: "Purify them." They all worked to this end and never despaired of success, as they had certainty that a treasure remained buried in people's hearts. Look, if you have a precious diamond and then it falls into the toilet, are you going to flush it down with the dirties? Would anyone suggest such a thing? Perhaps some proud or weak stomached people might call for a servant to do it, but no one in his right mind would flush it away. Then when you retrieve that diamond you are going to wash it with soap and water thoroughly, perhaps dip it in rose oil, and then return it to your finger. No one is then thinking that the diamond is dirty. Diamonds do not absorb the qualities of what they fall into – souls are the same.

In our time many people are searching for common ground upon which followers of all religions may stand, a school of thought that may trace its thread through all true inspiration. This is that common ground: aspire to a deeper understanding through your religion, and understanding that will open your eyes to the presence of the One in all things, that will reveal to you the respectability of all creatures, especially human beings, and enable you to desist from hating evildoers even while opposing their plots. This view will distance us from such a strong identity with labels that evoke fervor or enmity, such as: American, Russian, German, Turkish, Greek, Armenian, Jewish, Christian, Muslim, Buddhist, and draw us closer to the realization that our Lord has honored us all equally through the universal presence of His divine essence in our hearts. From that vantage point we will see that our Lord has given us through that essence wonderful and unique characteristics, made each and every one of us a manifestation of His divine attributes, of Himself.

Then it will be clear to us as well, that the veils of ego that cover our essence are as varied and subtle as the differences in the manifestation of the essence; every one has unique "ego traps" designed to catch his own unique soul – and to avoid or escape these traps is at the heart of the knowledge of the Way. Only the one who approaches his Lord with sincere piety may discover that way, and that sincerity is what our Lord desires of us, what is of real value, as He says in His holy book: "The best (or most honorable) of you is the most sincerely pious and God fearing." In other words, our Lord has honored us all, but reserves His highest honors for those who strive toward Him.

The Prophet Muhammad, upon whom be peace, was endowed with the widest understanding of the significance of the holy verse: "We have honored all of the Children of Adam", the understanding of the presence of the One in the many. Mawlana Jalaluddin Rumi was given the distinction of declaring these realities most openly to all Nations, inviting all people unconditionally through an open door, saying:

Come, come, whoever you may be,
come again.
And be you non believer, Magian or idolater,
come again.
Ours is not a Dargah of despair!
Though you may have broken your repentance a hundred times,
come again.

As Allah Almighty opens His doors to all His servants, so do we accept our Lord's servants. We are not fanatics who spend their lives interrogating those who seek to quench their thirst at the fountain. This is the way of our grandshaykh, who declared: "I am an advocate for all the Children of Adam on the Last Day." When someone arrives at our doorstep, we know who sent him, so we can't refuse.

113

Love is Lovely

Love is lovely to the Lord and to His servants. If you do anything with love, it will be accepted by your Lord and He will make it tasteful for you. If you love your work it will be easy for you to do, if not, it will only be a burden. The Lord says: "I am not in need of your worship, I am only seeking the love with which it is offered." Oh servants of the Lord, Oh believers, you must not overlook this point. Don't be like slaves rowing in the galley of a ship – if you pray, you must pray with love not by force, as if a slave driver were standing over you with a whip! Allah never appreciates such forced devotions. Now we are trying to perform all the practices but forgetting to ask for divine love, so we are becoming like mechanical robots, or like people performing gymnastics.

Allah has asked us to engage our bodies in His worship and in service to His creation through charity and good deeds, but what must be the fruit of those actions? If the fruit is not love it is a bitter fruit and is rejected. If our worship causes love of God to grow in our hearts, then we must keep to that practice and continue on our way; and if we are keeping the company of a spiritual teacher, and find that through keeping his company love of God is awakening in our hearts, then we must follow him closely.

The love of God is not easy to attain, for we cannot imagine Him; therefore, He Almighty has made the prophets apostles of His love. Allah's Beloved, the seal of prophets, Muhammad, upon whom be peace, was such a pure medium for the transmission of that love that the hearts of his companions were overwhelmed with his love, and were transported to the love of God. He was the representative of Allah, who is the Absolute Truth; therefore, the Prophet declared: "Who has seen me has seen the Absolute Truth."

When a delegation of non Muslims came to visit Medina, they were amazed at the love and respect shown to the Prophet by his companions. When they returned home they said to their leader: "We have met many emperors, kings and tribal chiefs, but never have we seen one whose subjects or courtiers treated him with such sincere love and devotion. How can this be?" They were not able to comprehend the secret of this love, as their egos caused them to deny Muhammad's prophethood. The love of the companions towards the Prophet was such that they used to say to him: "I am ready to sacrifice for you even my mother and father", which, for the Arabs, is much stronger than saying: "I would sacrifice myself for you." And in reality many of them underwent nearly unbearable hardships for the sake of their belief in the mission of the holy Prophet: exile, disinheritance, boycott, torture and death.

Who represented the holy Prophet after his life on earth? Those who evoked such love. The Prophet himself described them: "Those who see them are reminded of God." He who thirsts for divine love must seek out such people, but in our time they are mostly hidden, and Islam has come to mean for many people only a set of rules of conduct and forms of worship – an empty shell. Who can derive taste from such a thing? Shall mosques be only gymnasiums? And now the "gym teachers" are opposing Sufi Paths, which are the ways of the heart, ways that lead to the love of God.

Our Lord has given us an instrument that measures not our blood pressure but our "love pressure" and our goal is to make it high! Yes, seek to improve with every new day, for the holy Prophet said: "Whoever does not improve with each day is losing ground." What does this mean? It doesn't mean that if we pray forty rakats of prayer today, we would pray forty one tomorrow and forty two the next day. No, that is not required, what is required, what is intended is that you fill your worship with ever more love of your Lord, so that He will observe: "My servant has sent Me more love today than yesterday. "One of our grandshaykhs summarized perfectly what I am trying to say: "An atom's weight of love is worth more than seventy years' worship without love."

Love is the Mortar of All Prayer

As we were coming to the mosque today I saw a billboard that read: "Everyone Needs Standards." I didn't understand what this could mean, but just then the traffic light turned red, so that we stopped right in front of the sign. Then I looked more closely and noticed that someone had vandalized the sign, and with a pen had crossed out "Standards", and written instead: "Love not Standards", so that the billboard now read: "Everyone needs Love, not Standards."

If one is open to wisdom he may take wisdom from every side, and so, Glory to Allah, this bit of vandalism has given me a topic for this lecture. Yes, that person was right, and this recalls to mind a saying of the Prophet Muhammad, upon whom be peace, in which he prayed to God:

"Oh Allah, I ask You to grant me the love of You and the love of those whom You love, and grant me, Oh my Lord, the love of those actions which lead me to the love of You."

To ask our Lord to open up our hearts to His divine love is the most important request we can make of Him in our prayers, as nothing can take the place of love. The holy Prophet, who is called the Beloved of Allah, whom Allah created with the yeast of love, and whom Allah loved so much He dedicated the creation to him, even this beloved prophet asked Allah for divine love – why? Because who tastes of that love asks for more. Whose heart is like a rock will not ask God for this love, but those who have had the slightest taste of that love know that it is the key to all spiritual progress, to mercy, beauty, wisdom, to all favors that God may bestow upon His servants. Therefore, the holy Prophet taught all mankind what is precious in this life.

And then his prayer continued: "And grant me the love of those who love You." The first level, "love of God", is the station of the prophets, and you can't step from the bottom of the stairway to the top in one step. Allah Almighty is the Transcendent Being – you can't even begin to fathom anything about Him Almighty – but it is easy to love those who represent His love among mankind, for it is much easier for us to begin to understand and love human beings like ourselves. You will find nothing in their hearts but the love of God: therefore, loving them is a means to approach the divine love.

Lastly, the holy Prophet asks for the love of those actions which lead to the love of God, actions which carry blessings with them, which soften our hearts and weaken our greed and selfishness. These are the actions encouraged by our Lord through the example of His prophets, actions ordered and recommended in His holy books. And, although in the beginning our inner state may not correspond to these saintly actions, by engaging our limbs in what pleases our Lord, He will strengthen our hearts thereby.

These are the three levels of love for which the holy Prophet prayed, and the wisdom reflected in this prayer is proof enough of the veracity of Muhammad, peace be upon him. While Believers must always ask for that love, Satan is ever at war with such a notion, for he knows that once love has entered the heart of one of his slaves, that slave is lost to him, for he will not be able to snare him anymore with this world's pleasures. He who has tasted that love may not even notice those pleasures, or may regard them as only a drop in an ocean.

Once, as Moses, upon whom be peace, was headed toward Mount Sinai, he passed the cave of a hermit. The hermit emerged and called after Moses: "Oh Moses, please ask our Lord to bestow upon me just an atom's weight of His divine love." Moses agreed to do this, then continued on his way. Later, when Moses was addressing his Lord, he petitioned on behalf of that hermit. The

Lord replied: "I will grant that servant of My divine love, but not in the amount he requested. I will only grant him the tiniest fraction of an atom's weight of that love."

When Moses returned from the mountain, he quickly went to see what was happening to the hermit, to see what effect such a tiny dose of divine love might have had on him. When he arrived he was startled to see that where the cave had been a part of the mountain was blown away, and in place of that cave there was a deep chasm in the earth. "Oh servant of my Lord", he cried out, "what has happened, where are you?" Then Moses looked down the chasm and saw the hermit sitting down there as if in another world, completely overwhelmed by that love.

Why did that hermit ask for a portion of divine love? Because he was worshipping but feeling nothing; he felt an emptiness in his heart that could only be filled by that love. Without love, worship is tasteless and useless; therefore, we must be sure to build our worship upon a strong foundation of love and to bake love into the bricks of the building of our devotional practice. This is more than an analogy, for even physical buildings are either alive with the love of their builders, or dead from their hard heartedness. Therefore, old buildings often emanate a good feeling because of the love and goodness of those who built them. This is especially true of old mosques and churches, for their original congregations built them for the sake of their Lord's love and in an attitude of sincere piety. There is often a very strong feeling of the Divine Presence in old mosques, but have you ever felt such an atmosphere in the new showpiece – of – sterile – architecture – mosques? No, it is impossible; you may feel only an inner contraction inside of such concrete hills. They have left the love out of the mortar: the most important ingredient is missing.

He Who is Without Shoes,
Look at the One Without Feet!

Of all of our ego's characteristics, without a doubt envy is the worst, for an envious person, even if he were in paradise would feel himself to be in hell. And the irony of this characteristic is, that the more enviable positions people seem to attain in life, the more severely afflicted with envy they themselves become. Therefore, envy is most rampant among the rich and privileged who are disturbed by the fact that others may be even richer or of higher rank than themselves, and wish to be the only ones to possess everything. Common people do not envy each other as much as the upper classes do.

Yes, it is ironic that those who are more educated, who claim to have a better understanding than the masses should be blind to the harm they are inflicting upon themselves, oblivious to the fire that is rapidly burning them up. If they are so intelligent they should realize that their Lord brings people into this life and sets them in different conditions, and that despite the discrepancy in their outward ranks, all have been honored by their Lord and bestowed with dignity. Whoever has been favored with even the slightest degree of wisdom must know this and so be free of envy. God's holy prophets and their Inheritors, the Friends of God, have always reminded mankind of this fact: each and every one of them has been honored by being created as a human being, and need envy no one. Our Lord, in the holy Quran, encourages us to not only understand this point, but to declare it openly, when He Almighty says:

"(Oh people), proclaim your Lord's favors unto you."

We were nothing and our Lord brought us into existence; can there be any favor greater than this? And our Lord informs us that all things in existence are busy glorifying their Lord, even atoms. Atoms, too, have life, because without life it is impossible to be in existence. Perhaps we can say that the atom's life is of a very different kind from our own, but they are also perfect in their own right and are praising their Lord for the grant of that perfection.

Those who have attained certainty of faith, who have a light shining in their hearts, may perceive even inanimate objects glorifying their Lord. One of the miracles bestowed upon our Prophet Muhammad, upon whom be peace, was that, one day he held up a handful of pebbles and all those present were made to hear those pebbles glorifying their Lord. All of creation participates in this glorification: rocks, earth, water, plants, trees, leaves, flowers, fish, birds, ants, bees roam Allah's spacious earth, swim in His seas, fly in His skies, or to just be a part of that creation – all are grateful, except for dissatisfied mankind. The holy Quran states:

"Everything in existence glorifies Allah, you just don't understand their glorification", and also:

"Hast thou not seen how to God bow all who are in the heavens and all who are in the earth, the sun and the moon, the stars and the mountains, the trees and the beasts, and many of mankind? And many merit the chastisement: and whom God abases, there is none to honor him. God does whatsoever He will."

Notice that "some of mankind" is the only exception to the rule. This is because all of creation is obedient to Allah by nature, and only mankind has been presented with the option to praise the Lord and to find inner peace or to be ungrateful and live in the hell fires of discontent and envy. So what about you, oh ungrateful mankind? You may own a Rolls Royce and live in a splendid palace, but if you are ungrateful you are beneath the level of inanimate objects. And I am sorry to say that in our times widespread envy is destroying all humanity.

Nowadays, whoever is obliged to ride a bus is surely envious of car owners; and how should it not be so with spiritual values in such a state of eclipse? A medieval Persian Sufi poet, Shaykh Sa`adi Shirazi, wrote about a person who was so poor he was not able to afford a pair of shoes. This person used to complain incessantly about his condition, but the more he complained the less inclined anyone was to buy him shoes. One day he came across a person who had no legs, and this sight caused him to repent, saying: "Oh my Lord, thank you for giving me legs with which to walk!" Yes, we must consider the blessings we have been given.

The other day I visited a man who is waiting to die of a terminal disease, a disease that does not leave him either to eat or drink. If that person possessed all the gold contained in the Bank of England, do you not think that he would gladly give it all if he thought he could thereby prolong his life? Does anyone think that he would refuse? You must consider what you have been given! Would any of you agree to give me both of your eyes in exchange for all that gold, or even if, in exchange, I were to make you king of the world? (Now if I offered such power or wealth for one eye, so many foolish people would readily agree!) Of what use would that kingdom be to you then? You would be known as "the blind king."

But people are foolishly saying: "Why does that person own a Rolls Royce and not I? "Why does he live in a palace and I live in a flat?" "Why does he own a business and I have to work for wages?" "Why is that person a queen and I am a subject?" You must be thankful that Allah Almighty put Her Majesty the Queen on that throne! A wise man observed: "Allah has placed His slaves in the positions He has chosen for them."

One of history's most renowned Sufi Shaykhs, and one of the golden Naqshbandi chain of transmission, Abu Yazid al Bistami, Sultan al Arifin, was once passing through a narrow alley with his followers. All of a sudden a small dog appeared at the other end and was alarmed at the emergence of so many people; then Abu Yazid stepped aside in order to a let the dog pass, and his followers did the same. Someone said to him: "Oh Aba Yazid, you are a distinguished grandshaykh, and you are walking with your respectable entourage – how can you give way to a dirty dog?" Then Abu Yazid replied, and in his answer is to be found a lesson for all humanity: "Oh my sons, when that dog appeared and saw his way blocked by so many formidable figures, he said to me, 'Oh Shaykh, don't be proud of being a Shaykh and a man, thinking yourself above me in station. No, you must know that we are equals in creation, for it is only the Creator – yours and mine – who dressed me in the form of a dog, and I am grateful and pleased with my Lord. He dressed you in a human form; you didn't create it yourself, so don't be proud!' When it was addressing me in this manner I felt ashamed in front of my Lord and knew that it is wrong to look down on any creature, as it is Allah who created each one.

Once I was walking with our grandshaykh through the streets and noticed a rock lying in the road. Since it is a meritorious action to remove such obstacles from the way, I decided to move it, but being too lazy to bend down and take it away with my hand, I just kicked it aside with my foot. Then Grandshaykh reprimanded me, saying: "Oh Nazim Effendi, you must never do that again. You must consider Who brought that rock into existence, and so maintain for it proper respect."

Such vision is the vision of the People of Truth, those who have perfectly grasped the teachings of Islam, and that perfect understanding leads one to respect everyone and everything in existence. And if such is the level of respect maintained for a dog or a rock, what about our relations with our fellow man? How can envy thrive among real believers? It is impossible. But we are only imitators; that is why envy spreads through the world community like cancer through a body, and now that cancer is attacking individuals, nations and the whole world.

Know that it is only this rotten characteristic that is preventing you from attaining the breakthrough. Leave envy and you may approach your goal, and the nearness of Angels, prophets and the Friends of God.

Our Stand Against All Cruelty

Abu Yazid al Bistami, a giant among our grandshaykhs, once explained that Islam, in its essence, is built upon two great pillars; that everything we are exhorted to do or to believe in can be understood as falling into two broad categories. One pillar is the acceptance of Allah as our Supreme Lord, and our striving to both respect His exalted station and recognize our true position as His humble servants. The second pillar is our being merciful, our showing compassion towards all of God's creatures.

These two categories encompass every aspect of our lives; and when we evaluate our actions according to the spirit of these broad principles, we may derive benefit from Islam in the way it was intended.

Everything we do must be dedicated to our Lord: that is why we initiate all our actions with the invocation of His attributes of mercy, as Allah Almighty Himself invoked these attributes of mercy when revealing the first verses of the holy Quran (and when revealing succeeding chapters), by saying: "In the Name of Allah, Most Merciful, Most Beneficent and Most Munificent." Invoking these attributes of mercy is the key to success and the acceptability in the Divine Presence of our deeds of mercy towards our fellow creatures. You must always remain aware that without His divine help you can't succeed in any attempt at good actions. Indeed, without His support you can move neither hand nor foot.

Now that you have devoted your life and all of your deeds to your Lord, invoking always His attributes of mercy, you must strive to show pity to all creatures. And even if you need to kill any creature you must do so as painlessly as possible. That is why there is a very specifically prescribed method of slaughtering animals for food, a way that involves the least suffering for the victim. When we carefully observe that ancient method of slaughtering we incur no guilt, but now people are so careless and so heedless of these divine Instructions and of the suffering of the victim, that they risk being blamed by their Lord for their cruelty.

Even when exterminating harmful insects or animals, it is necessary to do so in the most painless way possible. And it is absolutely forbidden in Islamic Law to kill any living thing by fire. Allah Almighty has reserved for Himself the right to burn who has earned such a fate in the fires of hell: He Almighty has extended that right to no one else. It is forbidden to burn fields because of all the insects that are burned in the process, and most emphatically it is forbidden to kill any human being by fire. Neither is it permissible in the case of execution (No burning at the stake!) nor in the case of war (No guns, no bombs!). But now Nations are preparing to burn up the entire world with fire. All modern weapons are basically firearms: that is prohibited. First of all, it is only permissible to wage war when all attempts at a peaceful settlement have been exhausted, and then only with cold iron spears, swords, etc. Fire is only for cooking and heating.

We must be merciful. Don't even step on an ant without reason: it lives too and sees that you are approaching to kill it, feels fear and tries to escape. It feels pain and fears death; therefore it runs away. You must remember that it too glorifies the Lord, and so if it doesn't harm you, you mustn't kill it, and if you do you will be held accountable. The message of Islam is mercy for all creatures, and mercy is the underlying theme of the teachings of all Sufi teachers.

The Disappearance of Virtue
From the Face of the Earth

When the Angel Gabriel made his last visitation to the Prophet Muhammad, Peace be upon both of them, he informed the Prophet: "This is the last time I shall come to you with revelation, and, furthermore, with your passing, prophethood will be a closed book: no more will I come to earth with divine commands." The holy Prophet then asked him: "Is it really to be so that you, who have brought divine Guidance to Allah's prophets throughout history will never again visit the earth?" Gabriel replied: "Indeed I will return in accordance with my Lord's divine Command, not to deliver guidance, but to take back, one by one, all of the virtues that have flourished through divine Guidance. This is my Lord's plan: that the spiritual condition of mankind should deteriorate before the coming of the great events of the Last Times."

"First, I will come to take away divine knowledge, so that ignorance will cover the earth like an ocean, and the people of that time will fall into it in hordes. Those people will not declare, "There is no god but the One True God, Allah', but will claim, 'There is no God'. (This is the epitome of ignorance, for you may know everything, but if you don't recognize the Owner of all and the Creator or your own being, you are ultimately ignorant). Yes, I will come to remove the knowledge of all higher realms and leave them in the darkness of ignorance."

"Then, again I will come and take away "barakah"" (Barakah means being blessed by God with adequate sustenance, and consequently feeling contentment with our allotted portion). Nowadays, people's needs have proliferated to such an extent that no one can begin to possess a tenth of what they imagine themselves to need. Despite the fact that their pockets are bulging with money all they can be heard saying is: "Not enough, not enough." I can remember, during my childhood that people used to earn about three piasters a day – it was just a small silver coin. Now in our country I don't think that one can subsist on five pounds a day – and what about here in England! Yet, in countries where there are kings and queens there is still more "barakah" than in republics. There used to be shepherds who earned only one piaster a day plus food and shelter for themselves and their families, and they were happy – for what does a humble person really need beyond food, shelter and some money for clothing etc.? But those are bygone days... "barakah" has been taken up and people are swimming in an ocean of discontent.

Then Gabriel said: "I will come to take away mercy from the earth." For example, I saw in the newspaper yesterday that some people who looked like robots went on the rampage at a football game and killed many people. Surely their heads are like footballs, full of air, and their hearts like rocks, containing no mercy. This is but a simple example of how beastly man can become when there resides no mercy in his heart, and indeed, worse than beasts, for beasts kill for food, not for fun. Islam always opposes such barbarism, as our prophet is the Prophet of mercy; but look, in our time, two Islamic countries have been engaged in a useless, protracted and bloody war, mercy has been taken from their hearts as well, and they also can boast of having attached footballs to their shoulders where the head should be.

"And finally," continued Gabriel, "I will come to take away modesty and chastity." It is not difficult to see that this has been accomplished already. Nowadays, people walk the streets in attire that their mothers and grandmothers would have been ashamed to wear in their bedrooms.

And this is what the Angle Gabriel informed the holy Prophet of fifteen centuries ago, and he, in turn, informed us that the time we are living in is virtually bereft of the qualities that make human life human. And, indeed, we find ourselves living in such a time as he described. There is no more knowledge leading people to goodness, to honesty, to honor, here and hereafter. People are studying, but to what end? They are only learning to support the kingdom of Satan on earth, to help perpetuate that state of affairs that is rapidly bringing the whole world to the brink of disaster, and creating such alienation in people that so many would rather throw themselves out of windows than go on living, and so many others live only to inflict suffering on others. Even in religious schools, where the elements of godly living should be taught, that knowledge has been distorted out of recognition and soured, like a glass of milk into which a lemon has been squeezed, so that even those with a basis in divine knowledge can barely distinguish right from wrong anymore, what to speak of doing what is right.

Islam brought the world respect and mercy, but we have lost them both. And despite the odds we face, we must ever strive to develop those virtually extinct good characteristics in ourselves. And we are comforted by the knowledge that our Merciful Lord will not fail to judge us leniently, as we are trying our best to see something through the obscurity of these times, and we are looking for the light at the end of the tunnel.

The Heavenly Homeland

The homeland of the soul is the heavenly realm, just as the homeland of our human personalities is wherever we were born and raised. People have tried to describe the goal of the Sufi Path in so many ways, but the best description is to say that it is the way by which the soul may return to its homeland. Our souls long for that heavenly homeland, just as we may dream of returning to the scenes of fond childhood memories. That attachment to our childhood homes is a reflection of the soul's longing for its original homeland; therefore, its existence is a sign of faith, and the holy Prophet, peace be upon him in a tradition, is to have said: "Love of one's homeland is of faith."

Therefore, you may come to spend Ramadan here in London, and you may feel by the end of your time here a longing for your homelands. The same holds true for pilgrims to Mecca and Medina: Allah plants in people's hearts a love that enables them to bear all of the hardships of the journey and the pilgrimage, so that people may do their duty to their Lord: then He changes that longing for the holy places to a longing to return quickly home.

It is normal that a person should long for his homeland. We have a saying: "You may put the nightingale in a golden cage but it won't be happy, and will lament: "Oh that I were back in the nest I made from sticks and straw." One may see this in the community of our Cypriot immigrants here in London, or with other groups, that have come seeking "streets lined with gold." You may hear them moaning: "Oh our village, our mountains, our rivers, our seas, our old friends!"

That longing is only the longing of the personality and the physical body for a place it associates with good memories; but the longing of the soul goes much deeper. And just as it may sadden a person who returns to the home of his youth, and finds not there the people he loved, so, for the soul Heaven is empty without the countenance of the Lord. Foreign dignitaries don't go to Buckingham Palace unless the queen is there – for what should they go, otherwise for sightseeing?

And yourselves: you would not come to London to this humble place unless the person you love is here. Would you come from Canada to London for at least the fifth time to take a sightseeing tour? London is empty for you if that person is not here. But now London is full for you, and even if that person were to be sitting in a cave, London would be full for you because you have found that person. The longing of the soul is for its Lord: what is the divine realm without Him?

How the Ant With the Broken Leg Got to Mecca

Every person from among mankind may attain divine stations. The Way is not barred to anyone: we are all candidates for the position of "Deputy of God on earth." The holy verse is clear enough: "Oh man, verily you are striving towards your Lord, and you will meet Him;" therefore, whoever makes a serious attempt to reach, must reach. But if we consistently take one step forward and two steps back, and make ourselves fit Allah Almighty's description: "They believed, then fell into disbelief, believed again, and once more fell," then we will find ourselves lost.

Steadfastness is the quality that will aid our progress, even if that progress is slow. Be steadfast and you may reach your goal; and even if you don't, your Lord perceives your sincere intention and may convey you towards your goal, just when you have despaired. Our grandshaykh said that such perseverance in the face of immense odds is most difficult. Imagine that a person has been told: "There is a treasure waiting for you inside the earth, a fourth of the way to China – you must dig and take it. Here is a broken pick and a spade with a broken handle, now you may start digging." Imagine being ordered to such a task with such tools! You must start; don't say: "It is impossible! Even an oil drill can't reach down that far!" No, you must say: "My Lord has ordered me to proceed and He has given me these instruments with which to proceed with my task, so I must start digging." Then you dig, and when you collapse from exhaustion your Lord may deliver that treasure up to you in the blink of an eye.

Perhaps an ant with a broken leg may intend to travel from London to Mecca in order to perform the rites of pilgrimage. He may intend such a journey and start on his way, but do you think that there is any hope of him arriving? Allah Almighty sends a pilgrim who set down his handbag; as the ant crawls in to see if there is any food to be found for the way, the pilgrim comes, picks up the bag and gets into the taxi to the airport. When the pilgrim arrives at Jeddah, he boards a bus to Mecca, then a taxi to his hotel. At the hotel he leaves his other bags, but takes this valuable one with him to the holy Mosque to make his Tawaf of the Kaba.... After his Tawaf he sits down to read Quran, and the terrified ant slowly emerges, only to find himself in front of the Kaba.

Allah Almighty made a way for that ant because it firmly intended to reach that unattainable station, with its broken leg and all and he helped it arrive quickly, too. So don't lose hope! We are like that ant: we are directing our faces towards the Divine Presence and asking to attain to it. He may take us to that state, but we can never make it on our own.

Question: Is keeping our way in the non supportive surroundings of the West also like this?

Shaykh Nazim: These surroundings are like a whetting stone that serves to make our faith sharper and stronger. Our grandshaykh used to say to me: "Oh Nazim Effendi, if you can go to the downtown area of Damascus and return to this mountain without indulging your eyes, without casting your glance here and there, that is a greater feat and of more value than staying forty years in seclusion in a cave."

Yes, a man may go to Mecca and Medina for six months, fasting Ramadan there in the scorching heat and suffering thirst he never imagined when he fasted at home; he may stay through the Hajj season and experience overcrowded conditions unparalleled on the face of the earth. He may perform so many ritual prayers and rites with sincerity and may feel his faith renewed, but just as he is leaving the holy cities and their constraining atmosphere, and boards the plane at Jeddah, a seductive stewardess greets him, saying: "Welcome aboard...." Then his ego catches him and wrestles him to the ground.

Therefore, here in the West where conditions are difficult, you are offered the challenge of controlling your ego under conditions exactly contrary to those ends, but the reward is greater and of more lasting benefit. Here you may lose it all or you may reach your goal quickly. Yes, it is difficult to lead a chaste life under such circumstances, but you must not make excuses for yourself! You may live in surroundings that ensure that you are never for one moment allowed to forget sexuality, and you may feel that you will never be able to resist such an onslaught, but you must only intend sincerely to keep yourself and He will help you attain that goal – just remember the ant with the broken leg!

The Lion is a Harmless Pussycat, Until...

Allah Almighty sent every kind of trial to the holy Prophet and his companions – why? He Almighty willed that Islam become a great world religion, an international way of life, so He made sure to impart the perfect education to the Prophet and his companions, as they were to be the foundation upon which that great building – comprising all nations and races – was to rest. All training is based on trials, to ascertain whether each lesson has been well learned. One trial which Allah sent upon this first group of believers in Islam was hunger, since hunger is a powerful motive for our egos to rebel. People are very quick to anger when they are hungry; therefore, we have a saying: "The lion is a harmless pussycat – until it gets hungry!" When the lion is hungry it will attack, and the same is true of our egos. Whoever is able to control himself when hungry is proven to be trustworthy: whoever loses his self control at the first pang cannot be trusted.

The Prophet and his companions were tested in this way and found to be strong, and it was a training that helped them endure every hardship and keep their self control. Whenever the companions were hungry for three days the Prophet was hungry for four; when they were hungry for two days he was hungry for three. Once, when the Prophet has not eaten in three days, he went to Abu Bakr's house only to find that he had been hungry for two. Then both of them went to the house of Umar and found him in the same condition, but content and not complaining. How is it with us? If the meal arrives five minutes late we are disgruntled. With what right? Look, if a young lady says to her impassioned suitor: "If you remain two days without food I will come to you," he will say: "For your sake three days!" This is a simple example: if a young person may bear hunger for three days for the sake of the love of a creature, then why should we not be able to endure for our Creator, nay, even give our lives to Him, as He may make us content. With Him the thirsty knows no more thirst, the hungry knows no more hunger, the dead are no longer dead. That is the power of the love of God that has been transmitted to our heart.

Our brother here has opened his house to all of us: that is also a trial for him. It is impossible for the people of our times to have sixty or seventy guests in their homes. For our brother and his family this may be a spacious house, but such a throng must certainly be an imposition, and his welcoming us must be a sign of his strong faith. And if his house could accommodate one thousand people, his faith would cause him to open it to all of them, whether he knew them or not, as he only sees that they are all his Lord's servants. It makes no difference to him whether they are members of the Bundestag or peasants, Germans or Africans, because, through his faith, he has attained to the knowledge that the Lord is the Lord of the worlds, of all the Children of Adam, and that, as the Lord states in the holy Quran:

"We have honored all the Children of Adam."

Allah Almighty has respected us without distinction, and it is an attribute He calls on us to emulate.

Faith has settled in our brother's heart, so that he may take every burden upon his shoulders. Allah supports him and will provide, for whoever gives freely is never going to become poorer as a result of it. We are in need of such faith, for without faith our hearts become narrow and we can tolerate less and less the burdens we are asked to carry. But when we believe, our hearts expand and we can bear much joyfully.

And nowadays, when faith has been entirely lost, people cannot even bear the burdens of their own existence and commit suicide. The real cause of depression is only loss of faith. When faith is lost darkness descends on our hearts. We are in need of people who can bring the light of faith to people's hearts more than we are in need of psychiatrists to deaden people's feelings with their psycho Pharmacia. I am only a weak servant, and I am asking our Lord's help to bring us and the people of our time out of darkness.

The Source of Wisdom is the Heart, Not Any Book

A wise man may utter words of wisdom, but once they are recorded they join the body of knowledge that is generally available to listeners and readers far and wide. Once words of wisdom have been transferred to the realm of knowledge through such mediums as books and tapes, they lose something essential. Of course one may derive so much benefit from them still, but they can't replace the draught of wisdom from the gushing source – that source is the heart, and what comes from the heart of a wise man passes through his words directly into the heart of the seeker.

Where may one find wisdom? Not necessarily in the same place one would find a wealth of knowledge. A source of wisdom may be a Shaykh, a scholar or a professor, but may also be a plumber, a peasant or a totally illiterate person. Treasures are mostly sought in ruins, not in modern skyscrapers; buried under layers of debris, not sitting in the open, lying on the counter. And when the searcher finds some broken pottery or bits and pieces of a treasure that serves to enlighten him as to the realities of what he is excavating, he does not concern himself with the fact that these relics are not intact, for how could he expect to find that? And if you offer him brand new items from a supermarket that correspond in use to those ancient ones he found, he will not even consider your offer, and think you to be just joking, saying: "How do these two compare?"

Therefore, take wisdom wherever you may find it, and don't ask for titles or diplomas. Remember that your Lord may grant you wisdom through any means, so don't turn your nose up at anyone, but take a look at what he is offering, and if it be from ruins or in a ruinous state you must be ready to salvage it.

Wisdom belongs to the realm of the heart: once it has been grasped it is never lost. One of our grandshaykhs, Abu Yazid al Bistami, once addressed seekers of knowledge as follows: "Oh scholars, you are carrying your knowledge like a horse carries a load of books, you are loaded down and ever tiring, and you know that the holy Prophet said, 'Forgetfulness is the destroyer of knowledge'. As a termite comes and devours a piece of wood, so does time and age consume all you know. As long as you are in the hands of your egos your memory will decline with age, but the heart of hearts, once it has been awakened, strengthens with age. The heart is a source of wisdom that never dries up; but beware if you have not sought and received divine powers, for in the end your cup, which now runneth over will be as dry as a bone."

My grandshaykh, may Allah bless him, was over one hundred years old but his memory was remarkable. This wakefulness of mind was a result only of his spiritual condition, otherwise it would have been impossible.

As I meet more and more Westerners I find that they are very avid readers of books. I have never seen people who read so much! Centuries ago Muslims used to read, but now all that remains is that some people read the holy Quran, but when that practice is lost they usually stop reading altogether. But in the West, your hobby is reading, and perhaps, if you are seeking wisdom through books, you have asked yourself: "Perhaps I have read one thousand books, and I hope to read another thousand yet, but for what? To what end am I reading and reading and reading?" Then it may occur to you that you are seeking something else through your reading, something that reading draws you close to, but cannot get you to.

And when, as a result of this soul searching you begin to read from books of Sufi knowledge, of the Prophet, of Abu Bakr and Ali, of Rumi, of Attar, you only feel your longing more strongly and feel that you are even thirstier. Through all this reading you have tasted only a trickle, just enough to know how sweet a spring this is. By now you must realize that books are not the best vessels for wisdom of the heart, for the heart itself is the vessel, and the precious draught is passed from heart to heart. Where may such heart springs be found in a time that has turned verdant fields into desert wastes? Wandering through huge desert wastes, how many of us may just happen to stumble upon an oasis? First you may stumble upon one hundred mirages! But you must keep on, don't turn back saying, "I have found only illusions." No, no one said you have embarked on an easy journey, so you must be perseverant.

Because of the immense challenge involved in this quest for inner wisdom, for finding the bubbling spring in the desert wastes, so many people choose to totally ignore this most important facet of human life, and either devote themselves to the pursuits of worldly gain, or, if "religiously inclined", to the accumulation of religious knowledge. Imam al Ghazzali, a world famous figure in the history of Islam, was simultaneously a great scholar and a Sufi master. He wrote so many books that, to read all of them in a lifetime is challenge enough. It is said about his master work, "Ihya Ulum ud Din", "The Revival of Religious Sciences", that if all other books written by Islamic scholars throughout history were lost, this book alone would be enough to preserve all the essential knowledge of the centuries of Islam, and enough to keep Islam strong and vital. As his heart was opened to divine wisdom, he was able to expand our understanding of the holy Quran and the prophetic traditions through his writings.

According to Imam al Ghazzali, when a person dies, he is as a sleeper who has awakened. When he thus passes from the world of images to the world of reality, he faces immediately an evaluation of his time in this life. Even before he is buried in his grave the Lord will put forty questions to him. The first and most important of these questions is, "Oh My servant, during your life you were so careful to care for your appearance, to ornament yourself for the sake of your fellow creatures: wearing fine clothes, and arranging your hair. But did you bother to arrange your heart for your meeting with Me? You knew that I am not concerned with your physical beauty, the color of your hair or skin, or whether you are short or tall. You knew that I wanted from you only to purify your heart and to come to My Presence prepared, with your heart turned towards Me and not back to that place which you have left and which you knew you must eventually leave?"

In the holy Quran, Allah Almighty declares: "A man cannot have two hearts in the hollow of his breast." Therefore, the goal of all Sufi endeavors is to rid the heart of extraneous pre occupations, and turn towards Allah fully. This is the purification of the heart, and when this is accomplished, the light of Allah's Eternal beauty will shine on, and from the mirror of your heart. This is why, for those who have attained the inner reality to live up to such a practice, the meaning of fasting is not only what it implies, for the normal believer, i.e. abstinence from food, drink, indulgence and anger for a certain period of time, but the total absorption in the Divine Presence. Therefore, whenever a worldly whim seems to invade the heart of such people they consider themselves ritually impure and immediately take a shower. That is the level of saints, it is a practice impossible to be undertaken by others – we would always be wet. Yes, the Lord is calling us saying: "Oh My servant, why are you trying to escape from Me? If I were to leave you for even one moment you would cease to exist."

The Golden Chain of Spiritual Transmission of the Naqshbandi Khwajagan Masters

1. The Messenger of God,
   Prophet Muhammad ibn Abd Allah (ﷺ)
2. Abu Bakr as Siddiq (ر)
3. Salman al Farsi (ر)
4. Qassim ibn Muhammad ibn Abu Bakr (ق)
5. Jafar as Sadiq (ع)
6. Tayfur Abu Yazid al Bistami (ق)
7. Abul Hasan Ali al Kharqani (ق)
8. Abu Ali al Farmadi (ق)
9. Abu Yaqub Yusuf al Hamadani (ق)
10. Abul Abbas al Khidr (ع)
11. Abdul Khaliq al Ghujdawani (ق)
12. Arif ar Riwakri (ق)
13. Khwaja Mahmud al Injir al Faghnawi (ق)
14. Ali ar Ramitani (ق)
15. Muhammad Baba as Samasi (ق)
16. Sayyid Amir Kulal (ق)
17. Muhammad Bahauddin Shah Naqshband (ق)
18. Alauddin al Attar (ق)
19. Yaqub al Charkhi (ق)
20. Ubayd Allah al Ahrar (ق)
21. Muhammad az Zahid (ق)
22. Darwish Muhammad (ق)
23. Muhammad Khwaja al Amkanaki (ق)
24. Muhammad al Baqi Billah (ق)
25. Ahmad al Faruqi as Sirhindi (ق)
26. Muhammad Masum (ق)

27. Muhammad Sayfuddin (ق)
28. Nur Muhammad al Badawani (ق)
29. Shamsuddin Habib Allah (ق)
30. Abd Allah ad Dahlawi (ق)
31. Khalid al Baghdadi (ق)
32. Ismail Ash Shirwani (ق)
33. Khas Muhammad Ash Shirwani (ق)
34. Muhammad Effendi al Yaraghi (ق)
35. Jamaluddin al Ghumuqi al Husayni (ق)
36. Abu Ahmad as Sughuri (ق)
37. Abu Muhammad al Madani (ق)
38. Sharafuddin ad Daghestani (ق)
39. Abd Allah al Faiz ad Daghestani (ق)
40. Muhammad Nazim Adil al Haqqani (ق)

Lightning Source UK Ltd.
Milton Keynes UK
UKHW010623230919
350283UK00001B/29/P

9 781930 409057